In the beginning, God created the heaven and the earth. And the earth was without form, and void; and darkness was upon the face of the deep. And the spirit of God moved upon the face of the waters.

Genesis 1:1-2, King James Version

Upon the Face of the Waters

A BRIEF HISTORY
OF WAKULLA SPRINGS

Tracy J. Revels

Sentry Press
424 East Call Street
Tallahassee, Florida 32301

Front Cover: Aerial photo of Wakulla Springs and lodge. (John Moran, Springs Eternal Project)
Back Cover: The "Heron," one of Wakulla Springs river boats. (Bob Thompson)

This book is distributed by Friends of Wakulla Springs State Park.

For John Moeller

With love

Wakulla Springs offers a glimpse of primeval Florida where gators abound.
(Bob Thompson)

TABLE OF CONTENTS

A favorite photo opportunity in front of the historic bath house.
(Madeleine Carr)

Acknowledgments

No book is an island, and no author works completely alone. I would like to thank Dr. Madeleine Carr for her shepherding of both the original *Watery Eden* and this new, updated version. I would also like to thank the Friends of Wakulla Springs for their assistance in the book's publication, and for the wonderful work that they do in educating Floridians about nature's beauty and fragility. Bob Holladay of Sentry Press was also essential in making *Upon the Face of the Waters: A Brief History of Wakulla Springs* a reality, and Joney Perry deserves credit for her beautiful book design. Dr. Phillip Stone, Wofford College Archivist, provided advice and copyediting. My colleagues at Wofford College remain very generous in tolerating a professor whose mind is often wandering in the Florida wilds. As always, I would like to express my deep gratitude to my dissertation director, Dr. William Warren Rogers, Professor Emeritus at Florida State University, who inspired me to write the history of the place I loved, and to my mother, LaNora Zipperer, who inspires me in all aspects of my life.

Finally, I am most grateful to my husband, Dr. John Moeller, to whom this book is dedicated. We were married aboard the *Heron*, on the Wakulla River, on July 30, 2013. Wakulla Springs is a place that will always be special to us because our life together began upon the face of its waters.

Limpkins were once a common sight at Wakulla Springs.
(Bob Thompson)

Introduction

Wakulla Springs is a sacred place nestled deep in a primeval forest of cypress, live-oak, magnolia and pine. On foggy mornings, one can hear the sounds that were familiar to the First Floridians: the wail of a loon, the bellow of an alligator, the splash of a bass. By day, the great Wakulla spring offers cool comfort against the heat, and at night the fog returns, transforming the spring basin into a haunted cauldron, the grave of prehistoric beasts and the site of spirit revels. "An adequate idea of this mammoth spring could never be given by a pen or pencil," a visitor once wrote, "but when once seen, on a bright calm day, it must ever after be a thing to dream about and love."

Wakulla Springs is a crossroads, a place where man and nature have been meeting for thousands of years. When I wrote *Watery Eden: A History of Wakulla Springs* (the forerunner of this book), the spring was crystal clear, only occasionally darkened by naturally occurring acids during especially rainy seasons. Today, the spring is clouded and the glass-bottom boats no longer run. Wakulla Springs, a place I love with all my heart, has changed.

Change has been foreign to Wakulla. Much of its history is a story of how, over the centuries, people came and enjoyed the spring, but left it untainted. Plans for Wakulla's development were grandiose but unrealized. In the 1930s, the site was finally modified by a Florida businessman, who gave it a hotel and a fleet of river boats, turning a little-known local curiosity into a small yet classic Florida tourist attraction. The state's transformation of Wakulla

Springs into a state park in 1986 seemed to guarantee that it would be protected. But very little has protected Florida's wetlands from the byproducts of population growth and careless usage. Unless Floridians act quickly, and are willing to make sacrifices to save their precious natural birthright, Wakulla and other Florida springs will vanish into legend.

In my original introduction, I hoped that humanity would be "a little better" for having experienced nature at Wakulla Springs. Now it is time for humanity to return the favor — time to defend, protect, clean, and save Wakulla Springs, for truly there is not a moment to waste if Wakulla, that place to "dream about and love," is to survive. I hope that as you read Wakulla's story, you will be inspired to take up Wakulla's cause.

CHAPTER 1:
Mysterious Waters

A spring is a natural fountain that issues at the surface of the earth. It can range from a tiny trickle of moisture to a vast expanse of water that creates a river. Florida is blessed with over 900 springs, more than any other state. Each spring is an ecosystem, nourishing plants and animals. Each spring is fragile and beautiful, and all are endangered. None are more mysterious than the mighty Wakulla, located some fourteen miles south of Tallahassee, which bursts from its limestone cave to create the Wakulla River.

Wakulla is a first magnitude spring, meaning that it has an average flow of 100 cubic feet per second or more. Approximately 400 feet in diameter, Wakulla produces nearly 390 cubic feet of water per second for an average of 183 million gallons of water a day. The spring resembles a small lake and is surrounded by woodlands of pine, cypress, live oak, and magnolia. Like three other Florida springs (Weeki Wachee, Rainbow, and Silver) it is the principal source of a river, and its water temperature remains at a steady 68 to 70 degrees Fahrenheit year round.[1] Once privately owned, the spring is now the centerpiece of the Edward Ball Wakulla Springs State Park and is used as a tourist attraction. River cruise boats take visitors down the river and into a primeval Florida, where guests delight in the sight of manatees, alligators, and ospreys. Weddings and reunions are held inside the Wakulla Springs Lodge, and local children spend their summers daring each other to jump from the platform above the spring's deep maw.

But this is nothing new to Wakulla. Visitors have been coming here for almost 20,000 years.

. . . .

Two fountains originally gave Wakulla Springs its plural name. Located a little less than a mile northwest of the Wakulla Spring is Sally Ward Spring, which rises from a limestone shelf under the road leading into the park. The small spring has a run, visible from a footbridge, that winds down to the Wakulla River. The origin of the spring's name is uncertain. Local legend holds that it honors an African American woman who watered her cattle there, but other sources suggest it may have been named for a daughter of the Ward family, who owned plantations in the area. Nearby Cherokee Sink is a recent addition to the Wakulla Springs property.[2]

The exact origin of the word Wakulla is unknown. The spring was likely named by the Timucuan Indians, but their word and its definition were not recorded. The Spanish called the spring Guacara, while the Seminoles called it Wakala. *Kala* signified a spring of water in many Native American dialects, and a similar Creek word *wahkola* meant loon. Early cartographers used their imagination, naming the spring Talacatchina, Tagabona, West River, and Wachkulla. Variations on the spelling of Wakulla (such as Wakully and Wahkula) were used before the Civil War. Wakulla was adopted as the county's name in 1843. Though verifiable sources are lacking, many books cite Wakulla as meaning "the river of the crying bird" or "mystery." Boat guides have been known to refer to Wakulla as the "strange and mysterious waters," since, as Ranger Don Gavin stated on his tour, "we all know where this water is going, but nobody knows where it all comes from."[3] Considering the many mysteries of the spring and its past, this definition of Wakulla seems apt if not strictly authentic.

Wakulla's first visitors were the prehistoric animals that now rest beneath its waters. Divers have recovered bones of dozens of extinct species, including mastodons, mammoths, giant ground sloths, giant armadillos, bison, tapirs, and camels. Mankind arrived at Wakulla sometime during the Paleoindian Period (15,000 B.C. –

8,000 B.C.). Flint scrapers and bone fish hooks give insight into the lives of these First Floridians, who made seasonal migrations between water sources. During the Archaic Period (8,000 B.C. – 5,000 B.C.) the natives became more sedentary, and scattered artifacts and the presence of mounds on the property hint that the Wakulla River was an attractive spot for the seasonal and later permanent camps that would have been occupied during the Deptford (1,000 B.C. – A.D. 1) and Weeden Island (A.D. 500 – 1000) periods. The Fort Walton Period (A.D. 1000 – 1500) witnessed the first encounters between Native Americans and the Spanish conquistadors.[4]

Romantic legends credit Ponce de Leon with discovering the Wakulla Spring and hailing it as the fountain of youth. Historians, however, agree that the first European to reach the Wakulla area was Panfilo de Narvaez, who landed in Tampa Bay in 1528 and worked his way up the peninsula in search of the legendary province of Apalachen, which natives — no doubt anxious to send him packing — assured him was rich with gold. As his supplies dwindled, he was directed to the town of Aute, which he found burned, though he was able to snatch food from its abandoned fields. He then turned south toward the Gulf of Mexico, hoping for rescue by the ships he had dismissed in Tampa Bay. Starvation, disease, and angry Indians plucked away Narvaez's men, until a few hardy survivors constructed crude rafts and set sail for the Mexican coast. Eight years later, a ragged band of Spaniards reached Mexico City, among them Cabeza de Vaca, who penned the classic account of the doomed expedition.[5]

The exact location of Aute remains a tantalizing mystery. Cabeza de Vaca's memoirs can be compared with the journals of Hernando de Soto, who camped near the current site of the Florida capitol in the winter of 1539–1540. Though the two sources give slightly differing locations for Aute, modern archaeological work has narrowed the site to somewhere between Crawfordville and the Wakulla Spring. A 1993 dig on the south bank of the Wakulla River a quarter mile from the lodge yielded an array of Indian and Spanish artifacts, including earthenware fragments of Spanish olive jars typical of the containers that de Soto carried.

If Aute was a town on the Wakulla River, or even at the spring, it would make Wakulla the "Plymouth Rock" of the southern United States, the place where Europeans and Native Americans had their first well-documented interactions. But that premise raises a question: why did neither de Vaca nor de Soto mention the spring, which would have been crystal clear and certainly marvelous to Spanish eyes? And why have no bits of Spanish armor, weaponry, or tools ever been found in the park? Perhaps Aute was further away, and the artifacts arrived near the spring via trade, dropped and left behind by clumsy porters. One discovery could seal Wakulla's historical prestige. Cabeza de Vaca recorded that a Spanish boy who died on the expedition was buried at Aute. Should the grave of this young Spaniard be found by a future archaeologist, Wakulla's fame would be assured.[6]

The documented Spanish discoverers of Wakulla Springs were the priests and soldiers who arrived during the mission period, which lasted from the late sixteenth century to the early eighteenth century. Catholic priests celebrated mass with the founding of St. Augustine in 1565, and by the 1630s Franciscan friars were raising the cross in North Florida, throughout the region they called Apalachee. By 1676, there were a number of missions in the Tallahassee area, including one, Ascumpcion del Puerto, which may have stood near Wakulla Springs. Though no Spanish material of this period has been found at Wakulla, the spring was clearly familiar to the missionaries and their protectors, as it is referenced in documents and drawn (though unnamed) on a 1705 map.[7]

Spanish priests succeeded in teaching the Catholic faith, Spanish language, and European cultural traditions to hundreds of Apalachee Indians, as well as turning the Apalachee area into a reliable granary for settlements in Florida and Cuba. But the Spaniards were unable to make their charges a bulwark against the English aggressors to the north. Beginning in 1680, the Florida missions were harassed by Creek and Yamasee Indians who were being supplied and sometimes led by English colonists from Carolina. During Queen Anne's War (1702–1713), the Carolina Assembly commissioned James Moore to destroy the Apalachee missions and forts. With a force of some 50 colonists and 1,000 natives, Moore led two violent campaigns that razed fourteen missions and killed or enslaved over 10,000 Apalachee Indians.[8]

The smoldering fields of Apalachee gradually filled with a mix of Indian tribes dominated by the warlike Creeks. In an attempt to hold their territory and woo the natives, the Spanish opened a trading post at St. Marks in 1738. Meanwhile, a series of imperial wars weakened the Spanish, and in 1763, at the end of the French and Indian War, Spain was forced to cede Florida to England.

The new British overlords had little interest in colonizing Florida, preferring to govern through trade. Merchants from Georgia and South Carolina began bringing goods to Pensacola and St. Augustine. Among these entrepreneurs was William Panton, a Scotch loyalist who formed a partnership in Florida with Robert Leslie, eventually creating the firm of Panton, Leslie and Company, which would become the largest company engaged in trade with the southern Indians. Charles McLatchy, an associate, established a trading post on the Wakulla River in 1784, and this isolated outlet was one of the company's key storehouses. McLatchy soon connected with the Florida Creeks, who were now often referred to as Seminoles. The Wakulla River became a conduit of trade as the natives exchanged deerskins for guns, powder, blankets, iron pots, and rum.[9]

Spain recovered Florida through the 1783 Peace of Paris, which brought an end to the American Revolution. While most British subjects emigrated from Florida, Panton, Leslie, and their agents chose to remain, taking a simple oath of obedience to their new masters. Recognizing the necessity of warm bodies to hold wild lands, the Spanish government encouraged Americans and non-Catholics to settle in Florida and made Panton, Leslie and Company the crown's controlling agency on the frontier.

A colorful character had other plans for the firm. William Augustus Bowles, a native of Maryland who had married into a Florida Creek tribe, set up a ramshackle store near the mouth of the Ochlocknee River with the intention of giving Panton and Leslie some competition. With his Bahamian backers refusing to give him sufficient merchandise, Bowles concocted a very direct scheme for acquiring inventory. On January 16, 1792, Bowles and nearly 100 Indian followers arrived at the Wakulla store and demanded its wares. Approximately $15,000 worth of boots, guns, shirts and blankets were carried off by "that Villain Bowls" and his braves. Bowles fled, and after a series of misadventures that saw him imprisoned in jails literally around the world, he escaped and returned to Florida.[10]

Andrew Ellicott, an American surveyor hired to run a boundary line, encountered a shipwrecked Bowles on St. George Island in September 1799. Bowles foolishly bragged about his intentions to capture the Spanish fort at St. Marks; Ellicott felt he had no choice but to leave the vagabond stranded and report his dastardly plot to Don Thomas Portell, the commandant at St. Marks. Portell dismissed the threat, and Ellicott went on to make the first true scientific observations of Wakulla Springs. In April 1800, Bowles and the howling forces of "the nation of Muskogee" recaptured the hapless Panton and Leslie store on the Wakulla and laid siege to St. Marks. After a five-week standoff, Portell was forced to surrender.

Bowles's triumph was brief. A few months later, a Spanish fleet sailed in from Pensacola and bombarded the fort back to its rightful owners. Bowles fled, but was betrayed and died in 1805 at Havana's Morro Castle, in a room not far from where the inglorious Portell was being confined as punishment for losing St. Marks.[11]

The Bowles raid was the basis of claims against the Indians. In 1804, John Forbes, who was now the head of the distinguished firm (renamed the Forbes Company), acquired a cession of lands from Creek and Seminole chiefs. The immense tract stretched between the Apalachicola and the Wakulla Rivers and included islands in the Gulf of Mexico. The deal quickly became known as the Forbes Purchase.

John Forbes naturally wanted details on his company's new possessions and employed Asa Hartfield of South Carolina to survey parts of the purchase. While lots along the Wakulla River were marked off and their agricultural potential duly noted, Indian troubles and the War of 1812 kept settlers at bay. John Forbes read the American desire for Florida correctly and found a buyer for his extensive Florida holdings in Colin Mitchell, an American merchant in the Indian trade. Mitchell, in turn, gave tracts of land to his creditors in lieu of cash payments, and these creditors banded together to form the Apalachicola Land Company, an important force in Florida real estate as the territory passed into American hands as part of the Adams-Onis Treaty of 1819.[12]

Florida's cession to the United States came via a bloody struggle in the panhandle and on the heels of the execution of Wakulla's first famous resident. On November 30, 1817, Indians attacked and murdered a small party of Americans on the Apalachicola River. Known as the Scott Massacre, the event prompted Secretary of War John C. Calhoun to send General Andrew Jackson to chastise the natives and secure the area. Calhoun's orders were vague, and Jackson translated them as carte blanche to strike fear of the young American nation into the hearts and minds of the Spanish and their Creek and Seminole allies.

Leading a motley band of regulars, militiamen, volunteers, and friendly natives, Jackson crossed into Apalachee and on April 6, 1818, took the fort at St. Marks and established a base for strikes further into the interior. One of Jackson's targets was Chief Hillis Hadjo, a leader of the Red Stick Creeks. Known to Americans as Francis the Prophet, the chief was the founder of an Indian town on the banks of the Wakulla River. Francis was a significant figure who had once been taken to England by British agents and presented to royalty. His base on the Wakulla River was a strategic point for continuing agitation against the Americans, who had driven him from his Alabama home during the War of 1812.

Two former Forbes traders joined with Captain Isaac McKeever, who was paralleling Jackson's route along the coast, to lure Francis into a trap. They hoisted the Union Jack as McKeever's ship lay at anchor near the mouth of the St. Marks River. The ruse worked. Francis and another well-known Red Stick, Himmollemico, pulled alongside and accepted the friendly invitation to board. They were immediately overwhelmed and delivered as captives to Jackson.

7

Himmollemico, who had led the massacre of the Scott party, was quickly condemned to death, but Francis had his admirers even amid Jackson's crew. He was a man of intelligence and character, a "model chief" with pleasing manners, significant personal wealth, and an excellent command of both English and Spanish. Ironically, his daughter Milly had been responsible for saving the life of an American captive from Jackson's ranks. Despite his role as the stoic chieftain in the Florida version of the Pocahontas story, Francis was executed on April 18, 1818.[13]

Jackson's sanguinary exploits, which also included the executions of British traders Richard C. Ambrister and Alexander Arbuthnot, as well as the seizure of Pensacola, provoked an international incident that Secretary of State John Quincy Adams used as leverage to convince the Spanish to sell Florida. Jackson's mission also resulted in a remarkable and unfortunately obscure real estate brochure describing the Apalachee region, which would now be known as Middle Florida.

Captain Hugh Young, a topographical engineer from Tennessee, was instructed to prepare a report on Jackson's route. Young's *Topographical Memoir* commented on the soil, vegetation, geography, and Indian population from Pensacola to the Suwannee River. Young journeyed up the "Wakully" River to the spring and penned an account that would have whetted developers' appetites, had the report ever become public. Young described the land around the spring as second-rate but considered "the surface agreeably uneven and having charming spots for settlement." Unfortunately, Young's memoir gathered dust in the Army Corps of Engineers files for over a century.[14]

Florida was now open for American settlement, but a number of factors, including disputes over land ownership and the threat posed by the unconquered Seminoles, kept potential farmers and slave-owning planters cooling their heels in Georgia and South Carolina. The 1823 Treaty of Moultrie Creek, signed by 32 Seminole chiefs, supposedly pacified the region. Settlers were rightly wary, and they faced the further problem of inadequate intelligence about the territory. Where was the best land and where did the rivers run? The extent of the misinformation being circulated to potential pioneers is demonstrated in an 1821 map that shows the "Wackhulla" River extending all the way into Georgia and originating not in a spring, but rising from the tangle of the "Oke phanoke Swamp."[15]

Wakulla Springs had been a place of mystery for thousands of years. From the Spanish conquest of the 1500s to the American shoving match in 1818, Wakulla Springs was isolated and unknown to most explorers, seen only by natives, missionaries, soldiers and merchants who passed by it on their way to greater adventures. But with Florida's acquisition by the United States, Wakulla Springs would rapidly pass from uncharted obscurity into very public knowledge.

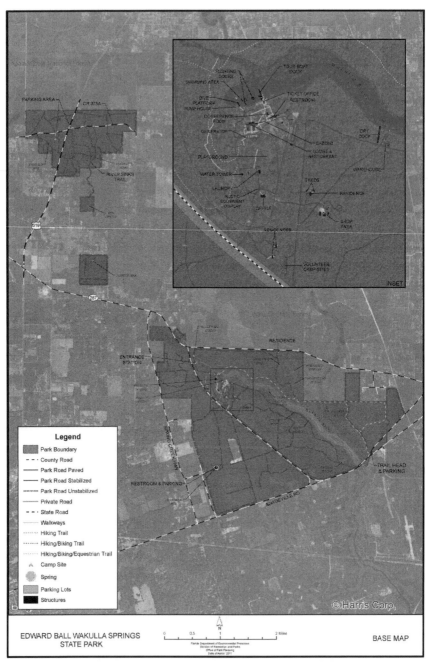

Extent of the state park's 6,000 acres in 2016.
(Florida Department of Environmental Protection)

General Andrew Jackson, whose 1818 expedition to Spanish Florida included the capture of St. Marks and a topographical survey of Wakulla Springs. (State Archives of Florida)

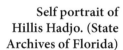

Self portrait of Hillis Hadjo. (State Archives of Florida)

Manatees in the Wakulla River. (Patty Wilbur)

CHAPTER 2:
A Wild and Beautiful Spot

Geography has tied the history of Wakulla Springs to the history of Tallahassee. The first promotional literature for Wakulla came as a result of the 1823 expedition that selected Tallahassee as the site of the territory's capital. Within a decade, Wakulla Springs was a popular local attraction, inspiring scientists, poets, and entrepreneurs in nearly equal measure. Everyone seemed to have plans for the springs, yet somehow these plans never came to fruition. With the possible exception of a few local boatmen, no one seemed to profit from the natural wonder. For almost a century, Wakulla belonged to individuals, but also to everyone, an unclaimed jewel in the Florida wilderness.

. . . .

During the British period (1763–1783), Florida had been divided into East and West Territories, with capitals at St. Augustine and Pensacola. Upon American annexation, meetings of the Territorial Council alternated between the two former capitals, an arrangement that delegates quickly found intolerable. Territorial Governor William P. DuVal appointed two commissioners to investigate the area of Middle Florida and choose an appropriate site for a new seat of government somewhere roughly between the former capitals. Dr. William Simmons, a St. Augustine physician, and John Lee Williams, a Pensacola lawyer, departed from their respective communities in October 1823. Williams, who was travelling eastward by ship, missed the initial rendezvous and decided to use his extra time to explore along the coast.[1]

13

On October 25, Williams and four companions took a small boat and ascended the Wakulla River to its source. Williams was astonished by the spring and took detailed notes on it. His observations appeared in published diary excerpts, his commissioner's report, and in two books, *A View of West Florida* (1827) and *The Territory of Florida* (1837). Williams reported that the river was navigable though obstructed in places by islands and river grass. He highlighted the "troops" of fish and the jagged ledge of the underwater cave. In Williams's view, the "Wakully River, rising from the earth, presents the finest spring in West Florida; probably in the world." He envisioned a bright future for Tallahassee, which he and Simmons selected as the capital, and for the Wakulla Spring: "Indeed it will not be presumption, to anticipate the time when the great fountain of Wakully will become the Arethusa if not the Helicon of Florida."[2]

Williams was not the only Florida promoter with an early interest in the Wakulla Spring and River. America was swept with a canal-building craze in the early 1800s. This fever reached Florida in the Territorial Period. In 1828, a number of Tallahassee notables, including future territorial governor Richard Keith Call, organized the Ochlockonee and Lake Jackson Canal Company, proposing to connect these bodies of water and then extend the canal to the Wakulla River. Permission to use any lakes or ponds necessary for the project was granted, but like many grandiose dreams of the Early National Era, this one quickly faded. Not a shovelful of earth was removed.[3]

Even without canals, Tallahassee was thriving. The first settlers arrived in 1824, and the capital quickly became a cacophony of political quarrels, whirling saw blades, minstrel music, and boisterous land speculation. Stores opened, churches were founded, and citizens prided themselves on their hospitality to strangers. Independence Day and Washington's Birthday were celebrated with public feasts. May Day tournaments and circus performances were annual civic treats. But even as the capital thrived, Tallahassee residents remained embraced by nature at her wildest, and many early settlers came to appreciate the untamed beauty of the Wakulla Spring.[4]

In 1829, a writer for the Tallahassee *Floridian & Advocate* penned a tribute to Wakulla laced with the classical allusions that all men of education (and pretension) enjoyed employing. He believed that the Wakulla and St. Marks Rivers realized the fable of Alpheus and Arethusa. If the Greeks had springs as great as the Wakulla, they could be forgiven their myths, for it was only natural to imagine gods, goddesses, and nymphs cavorting in the crystal clear waters. "Were it not for this unfortunate matter-of-fact generation we live in," the writer sighed, he "would be tempted to imitate the sages of yore, and celebrate the scenes by the Wakulla fountain." Pragmatic scientists had rather ruined the myth-making for him. Still, the Wakulla Spring was "a wild and beautiful spot," well worth the long ride from Tallahassee to its shore.[5]

Another early endorsement of the Wakulla Spring came from professional traveler Charles Latrobe, the author of *The Rambler in North America*, who visited in 1833. After a disappointing day in St. Marks, which was filled with dilapidated houses and uncouth residents, the great spring came as a pleasant surprise. "The source of the Waculla forms a large circular basin of great depth, in which the water appears to be boiling up from a fathomless abyss, as colorless as the air itself," Latrobe wrote. Latrobe was a detached, scientific observer, but also enough of a romantic to admit that Wakulla could easily have inspired the fountain of youth.[6]

Antebellum armchair adventurers could be further entertained by the detailed description of Wakulla that appeared in *Letters on Florida* (1835). Following chapters on history, geology, and agricultural products, the anonymous author turned to the territory's natural wonders. "But the most singular of all — the greatest natural beauty, and I may say, the greatest curiosity of the whole South, is the source of the Wahkula....This lovely sheet of water is 120 yards in diameter — so still and of such perfect transparency, that the smallest object is seen at the immense depth of the water below; and the spectator upon its surface, sits and shudders as if suspended in empty air." This sensation, of floating weightless on air rather than water, was common to almost all reports on the spring. Apparently, no visitor could resist the urge to push out over the spring in a vessel, though how these crafts were so quickly acquired is unmentioned. The author of *Letters on Florida* also speculated on the spring's future, when "these banks will be studded with private residence, as indeed even now the country round it is full of plantations."[7]

Surprisingly, no developer seemed anxious to make this scheme a reality. Though owned by the Apalachicola Land Company, the Wakulla headwaters and the land around it remained unexploited, essentially in the public domain until 1859. Picnics and pleasure trips comprised the primary usage of the spring, and the completion of the Tallahassee-St. Marks Railroad in 1836 made such day trips much easier. But throughout much of this period, a trip to Wakulla Springs involved a fair amount of risk, due to the ravages of the Second Seminole War.

The conflict began in 1835 with the massacre of Major Francis L. Dade and two companies of U.S. Army troops in a hammock near the site of present-day Bushnell. Though most of the fighting took place in eastern and southern Florida, Middle Florida (the region between Jackson County and Alachua County) was plagued with guerilla raids, which sent residents scurrying into towns for safety.[8]

Two explorers — one a scientist and the other a wandering clergyman — risked their lives to enjoy the Wakulla Spring during the Indian war. Francis de la Port, Comte de Castelnau, was a French naturalist. He mustered several boats and an armed escort before setting out from St. Marks on February 18, 1838. He sounded, measured, and even tasted the Wakulla Spring, along with recording the variety of wildlife he spotted along the river. His small expedition camped overnight, and while no Seminoles appeared, the men were uncomfortably aware of being on contested ground.[9] The clergyman, who is unidentified, reported his adventure in the *Knickerbocker* magazine in August, 1841. A talented storyteller, he recounted a morning of mishaps followed by an afternoon of delight with his soldier escorts at the Wakulla Spring. "Picture to yourself a RIVER leaping out of the earth at a single bound, and running off like mad in a current a quarter of a mile wide, and at the rate of four knots an hour," he exuded. "And altho your imaginary painting will come far short of the real scene, yet it will incite in you something of the wonder with which one actually beholds THE WAKULILA."

The soldiers found a boat and the pastor pushed off with them for a better view. The crew estimated the spring to be 120 feet in depth and the mouth of the cave nearly 50 feet in diameter. The poor "modest fishes" had no privacy and an angler could drop a hook right in front of his dinner's scaly nose. A long-running Wakulla tradition was established when a silver coin was dropped to the basin's floor. The soldiers claimed they could read the coin's date, but the honest reverend admitted, "that I *did not see!*"

The minister's trip ended abruptly when the stillness of the forest made the soldiers nervous. A mad dash allowed them to reach the train for Tallahassee before darkness closed in. The preacher's final evaluation reflected the tensions and prejudices of the time: "The Wakulila is one of the lions of Middle Florida" which "will attract many visitors into the country as soon as we shall be rid of certain other wild animals."[10] The Second Seminole War ended in 1842. By 1843, the Wakulla Spring was safe to visit, and its fame was rapidly spreading.

The first documented attempt to use Wakulla Springs as a tourist attraction surfaced in an advertisement in the Tallahassee *Star of Florida* on May 25, 1843. P. Randall, who resided a short distance from the spring, reminded subscribers of the "great natural curiosity" which was receiving large parties of visitors on a regular basis, now that hostilities with the Seminoles had ended. Randall announced he had "launched a new boat on the placid waters of the spring, on which visitors may be accommodated with safety." He also offered room and board for tourists, promising "every exertion will be made to render their visit pleasant and agreeable." His charges would be "modest." Randall did not own the Wakulla Spring, and his advertisement appeared only once, hinting that his business did not thrive as expected. His mention of a safe boat leads to obvious questions. Who was taking visitors over the spring? How often did accidents occur when a tourist leaned over the side for a closer look?[11]

The 1850s saw further publicity generated by articles in the

Tallahassee newspapers and regional publications. It seemed that everyone with literary ambition or scientific curiosity who visited the spring wanted to write about it. Sarah A. Smith, a young woman with a surprisingly good grasp of paleontology, travelled to Wakulla with friends in 1850. In her May 25 article in the Tallahassee *Floridian & Journal*, she correctly identified the scattered bones on the spring basin as those of a mastodon. Afterward, Smith and her friends engaged in dreamy fantasies about how they could stay at Wakulla Springs forever. One girl proposed that they change themselves into fishes, while another suggested setting up housekeeping in a floating castle. They finally agreed that to simply live along the river's shores would be enough.[12]

Increasing interest in Wakulla and other Florida springs was also evident in two articles published between 1851 and 1855. The journalist for the *American Agriculturalist* noted that a "singular feature of the country is full sized rivers rise suddenly out of some cavern of the earth, and lakes and streams in other places send their waters down into the earth." *DeBow's Review* highlighted the Wakulla Spring and speculated on the color of its water and the nature of its vertigo-inducing clarity. At the time, the spring was so clear that "attempting to analyze the unfathomable depths below, one beholds the clear and perfect reflection of the heaven's concave, with clouds flitting across its field, as it were a transient breath upon the surface of a faithful mirror."[13]

A literary visitor during the 1850s was Charles Lanman, whose *Adventures in the Wilds of North America* appeared in 1856. Lanman placed the Wakulla Spring beside Niagara Falls, Mammoth Cave, and Tallulah Chasm in his list of natural wonders. Lanman described the spring eloquently and declared that fishing within its waters would be a desecration. He also suggested that the river was wide enough for a steamboat, a comment perhaps inspired by observation of canoes and flatboats at work on the Wakulla.[14]

On the eve of the Civil War, a correspondent for the Charleston *Daily Courier* who went by the byline of "Batchelor" made a tour of the South, reporting on his travels with wit and style. His article on Tallahassee included notes on Wakulla. "Dropping a dime into the Wakulla is the customary tax upon the hidden mysteries. The little coin twirls as it continues to go — yet for seconds you watch its descent through the crystal liquid. Ours, we suppose, [must] have gone to China, for we never saw it stop."[15]

Just before the Civil War, the Wakulla Springs property was sold. S. Burton Ferrell, a Wakulla County planter, purchased the land around the spring from John Beard, the Receiver of Lands for the now bankrupt and dissolved Apalachicola Land Company. Ferrell paid $354 for an unspecified amount of property that included the spring. Though the Wakulla Spring was now technically part of Ferrell's plantation, there is little evidence that Ferrell removed it from public usage or profited from it. However, turpentine camps were being operated in the area, with or without Ferrell's knowledge. Archeological work, which has recovered buckets and bottles, along with local oral tradition and a Civil War era map, indicate that the Wakulla Springs property was active in producing turpentine from the mid-nineteenth century to the early twentieth century. Moonshining may also have been a lucrative (if illegal) enterprise at the springs.[16]

The Civil War brought an end to the first period of Wakulla Springs as an American wonder and natural curiosity. The war disrupted economic and social life throughout the South, though people in Leon and Wakulla counties were shielded to a degree by their region's natural bounty and great distance from the battlefields. Union raids on coastal saltworks were common, but for most people life would have been little changed except by high prices, lack of manufactured goods, and the volunteering or conscription of men into Confederate service. Taylor County's swamps became notorious havens for draft dodgers and army deserters. Perhaps some of these desperate men and their families also hid along the Wakulla River, enjoying fresh water and good fishing as they took care to avoid Confederate authorities.[17]

On March 5, 1865, a Union raid was launched from St. Marks with the goal of capturing Tallahassee. It was turned aside the following day by a combination of home guards, militia, and West Florida Seminary cadets at the Battle of Natural Bridge. Tallahassee citizens rejoiced, hailing the "Cradle and Grave" defenders as warriors of almost supernatural valor. But just a month later, the Civil War was over with Lee's surrender at Appomattox. Florida, like the rest of the South, was left with a crushed economy and a new social system. Increasingly, Floridians would seek ways to set their state apart. They began to use Florida's greatest natural resource — its semi-tropical climate — to their best advantage.

Wakulla Springs would be a part of this story.

The primitive conditions of Wakulla Springs before its development as a tourist attraction are suggested in this photograph, taken sometime around 1900. (State Archives of Florida)

Wakulla Turpentine Company on the Wakulla River in 1924.
(State Archives of Florida)

Anhinga dries its wings. (Bob Thompson)

CHAPTER 3:
Develop and Beautify

Tourism began in Florida in the 1820s with the territory's acquisition by the United States. The peninsula's first winter visitors came to recover their health. Suffering from consumption (tuberculosis) and other respiratory complaints, these invalids made arduous journeys to St. Augustine, Key West, Pensacola, and St. Joseph, hoping that the "salubrious air" of Florida would restore them.

Though they lived far from these famous resorts, citizens of Tallahassee and residents of Wakulla County recognized the potential for a spa in their own back yard. Wakulla Springs could become a resort, a place to rest or swim or even dance. For nearly a century, Wakulla Springs would attract speculators, promoters, and dreamers who saw in it an economic boom for the old Middle Florida region. Yet it would take the arrival of a Virginia entrepreneur, the last of the robber barons, to transform Wakulla Springs into one of Florida's classic tourist attractions.

. . . .

Health was always on the mind of nineteenth-century Americans, and for wealthy citizens relaxation and recovery were linked to social status. While most Floridians had to content themselves with visiting relatives or perhaps taking in an energetic camp meeting as a holiday from their labors, the smart set of antebellum Middle Florida frequented a number of resort establishments in the region. Before the Civil War, Bel Air (just south of Tallahassee), St. Marks, and Suwannee Mineral Springs had all developed reputations as watering holes where people went not only to relax, but to see and be seen. P. Randall, the first owner of the Wakulla Springs property, probably hoped to turn his home into a similar type of recreational establishment in 1843. Though his enterprise failed, the idea of Wakulla Springs as a resort had been firmly planted in the minds of locals.[1]

In 1858, a correspondent for the Tallahassee *Floridian & Journal* expressed frustration with his fellow southerners who travelled north to Saratoga Springs and other spas when (in his opinion) equally pleasant attractions were available much closer to home. He directed his readers to the facilities at Newport. While Wakulla Springs was still undeveloped, vacationers at Newport probably included it in their day trips. Commerce was common along the Wakulla River, and by the Civil War era the entire region was familiar with Wakulla Springs's beauty and novelty.[2]

During Reconstruction, the Wakulla Spring changed hands. On June 5, 1871, S. Burton Ferrell sold two plots of land to his son-in-law, J.W. Dugger. The spring itself was included in the bargain, and the property cost Dugger $111. Dugger, or perhaps a son, became the official attendant at the spring. In 1873, the Tallahassee *Weekly Floridian* noted that Westley Dugger "is provided with several good, safe boats and is always on hand to accommodate private and picnic parties with a row over the bosom of the spring."[3]

Floridians of the late nineteenth century became much more intentional about promoting tourism. With the development of steamboat lines and railroads, Floridians marketed their state to Yankee investors. Many areas in the state, including Silver Springs, had already become nationally famous. The Civil War had exposed people to Florida's bounty, and some northern transplants — such as Harriet Beecher Stowe, who bought a home in Mandarin — became vigorous advocates of Florida travel and living. For a state still economically depressed from the war and desperately in need of residents, the accommodation of tourists was not only a lucrative business but also a lifeline to the future. Though invalid travel was declining in the post-war era, wealthy sportsmen and captains of industry were easily lured southward.

As early as 1873, the *Weekly Floridian* commented on the northern desire for southern resorts, including "sanitariums" for rest cures. In 1874, Ellen Call Long, the daughter of Florida territorial governor Richard Keith Call, took up this suggestion in a series of articles on Florida history. She described the wonder of the Wakulla Spring (which she referred to as the Ponce de Leon fountain) and advised that the best time to visit it was on "a still sunshine day, without breeze, and with the sun as near his meridian as possible." A miracle equal to Wakulla's beauty was that "some enterprising Yankee has not discovered so eligible a spot for a Winter Palace Hotel."[4]

Meanwhile, the extended Ferrell family swapped and sold land following their patriarch's death. On December 27, 1875, J.W. Dugger and his wife sold a parcel of approximately 27 acres to W. W. Casseaux, another Ferrell son-in-law, for $300. Casseaux purchased two more plots of land from the Duggers in 1879. This $200 purchase included a 100 acre plot in the immediate vicinity of the Wakulla Spring.[5]

Travel articles and Florida guidebooks of the 1870s publicized Wakulla Springs as a scenic location, but also bemoaned the lack of facilities for the comfort of tourists. Wakulla was often mentioned in the same breath as Newport, which was still considered a resort for invalids. Perhaps young people ventured to the spring while their less rambunctious elders stayed in rocking chairs on the porches of their coastal cottages.[6] In 1882, artist Frank Taylor and author Kirk Munroe visited Wakulla Springs, along with a reporter from the Tallahassee newspaper. Taylor made sketches while Munroe soaked up the atmosphere for a future novel. Taylor pronounced Wakulla "more interesting than Silver Spring" due to its greater depth and larger alligator population. In the article about their trip, the local reporter commented on the lack of a good hotel. Wakulla Springs needed only "some better and more expeditious means of reaching it to add immensely to its attractiveness."[7]

In 1882, Wakulla's long-awaited resort came closer to being a reality when the spring was purchased by a Cincinnati physician and his wife. W.W. Casseaux sold several plots to Caroline A. Slosson, was who acting for her husband. Dr. M. H. Slosson was seeking a location for a winter sanitarium for his patients. For $88 and a pair of promissory notes, the doctor obtained 245 acres surrounding the spring. He announced that "improvements" would begin in the fall. The Tallahassee *Weekly Floridian* offered assuring words from the new landlord to locals who feared that a private hospital would cut off their access to the spring: "We understand that Dr. Slosson regards the 'old fountain' as still belonging to Wakulla County, and the fact of his becoming its proprietor shall in no wise hinder its use in the future, as for so long in the past, by the good people of that county as the scene of their annual May Fest."[8]

The Slosson sanitarium was not the only proposed commercial usage of the spring in 1882. *Florida*, a publication on the state's industry, agriculture, and commerce, noted that the native saw-palmetto plant could be manufactured into paper. Palmetto paper could be washed without damage and was impervious to alcohol. A "Professor Herring" had analyzed the water of the Wakulla Spring and "pronounced it well suited for manufacturing and bleaching palmetto paper." But despite this industrial promotion, no paper mill was built in the area, nor was any water diverted.[9]

Slosson's sanitarium project likewise floundered, with no construction occurring at the spring. In 1885, the *Weekly Floridian* published a letter from an unnamed railroad developer who had visited Florida for his health. He made no mention of a hotel or resort close to the Wakulla Spring, which he felt "bears about the same relation to all other springs I have ever dreamed of, that Niagara does to a canal lock or beaver dam." Unable to rent a room, the traveler prepared for a future visit by burying a bottle of wine on the riverbank and carving his daughters' names into a magnolia tree.[10]

As the region waited for development, Wakulla County citizens continued to use the spring as the site of springtime events, most notably the annual picnic which was held on the first Saturday in May. This custom, which was possibly rooted in the African American celebrations of emancipation on May 20, began in the 1870s, and by the 1880s was regularly announced and reported on in the Tallahassee newspapers. The community picnic offered free fish, bread, and coffee, supplemented by the contents of overflowing family baskets, and activities included games and boat rides over the spring. By the end of the century these picnics had also taken on political overtones, with candidates expected to make speeches or even announce for office at the event. Partisan tempers sometimes spoiled the fun. The *Weekly Floridian* reported on a brawl at the 1891 picnic, but was unable to offer reliable information as to either the participants or the outcome.[11]

In 1886, Dr. Slosson finally relinquished both his dream of a sanitarium and his Wakulla holdings. On April 7, Slosson and his wife sold land near the Wakulla Spring to C. G. Hubert of New York for $4,150, an impressive profit on such a small investment. Thomas B. Ferrell, son of the original owner, led a legal challenge to the sale, but the court ruled in favor of the Slossons. The Slossons also deeded just over 233 acres of their Wakulla property to their daughter, Florence Slosson Phillips, who transferred her interest in the land to her husband, Henry D. Phillips of Indianapolis. This transaction occurred in 1907, but following an apparent rift in the marriage, Henry Phillips sold the land back to Florence, subject to a mortgage held by Hubert. In 1915, Florence Phillips acquired almost 27 acres of property from Emily Thomas, the widow of John L. Thomas, and later that year she also acquired the acreage that her family had passed to C. G. Hubert in 1886.[12]

The sale and transfer of the Wakulla Springs property meant very little for the area's economic development. A geological survey of the Wakulla Spring in 1913 listed its uses as "none." In 1919 and 1921, the Bonheur Development Company sought oil in Wakulla County, sinking wells in locations outside of the Wakulla Springs property. Unsubstantial amounts of crude were pumped from the ground and the company soon abandoned operations.[13] The only documented use of the area around the Wakulla Spring was made by the Wakulla Turpentine Company, which leased the property from Florence Phillips for five years. Despite serving as the secretary for the Tallahassee Boosters Club, Florence Phillips was reluctant to accept challenges to "develop and beautify" her Wakulla Springs property.[14]

Competing forces of the 1920s shaped community opinions on the fate of Wakulla Springs. For most locals the spring itself remained a hidden treasure, visited by brave young people who endured the long and bumpy buggy ride from Tallahassee and never "went to Wakulla Springs without coming back engaged." For local African Americans who were "always available," these tourists provided supplemental income when they hired the men to row them over the spring. But this unofficial, unsanctioned tourism was being challenged by events occurring elsewhere in the state. The great land boom of the 1920s was enriching South Floridians while leaving North Floridians economically depressed, and many residents viewed developments lower in the peninsula with envious eyes. Some called for more development, including the exploitation of local natural wonders, to rival the sudden growth of Miami. But others were just beginning to realize the potentially destructive nature of unregulated commercial exploitation. In 1918, Henry Beadel took a canoe trip up the Wakulla River and described the Wakulla Spring with one word — "Paradise!" But could such a paradise survive if it fell into the hands of Florida promoters?[15]

Wary of this "greed of commercialization," Joseph S. Davis of Albany, Georgia, was the first to propose that Wakulla Springs receive government protection. Impressed by the site during a 1923 fishing trip, Davis composed an editorial for the *Albany Herald*, describing Wakulla Spring as a place "which abounds in cozy corners and shady nooks that shut out the prying eye of curiosity." He urged Florida's congressmen to take on the responsibility of inducting Wakulla into the National Park system to preserve its splendor for generations. His pleas went unheeded.[16]

In 1925, Wakulla Springs was purchased by George T. Christie, a Jacksonville real estate developer. He bought Florence Phillips's entire holdings. Rumors flew that he had paid $35,000 for the property. The actual price was $14,000. Though Christie made no immediate announcements concerning his plans for Wakulla Springs, imaginations ran wild in Tallahassee. In a *Daily Democrat* editorial, Mary Caverly conjured a fantasy scenario straight out of *The Great Gatsby*, with buses from Tallahassee making hourly runs to Wakulla, where stylish citizens would watch motor boat races and hot jazz music would float out into the moss-strewn trees from a brilliantly painted dance pavilion on the spring's shore.[17]

The backwoods casino failed to materialize, and local residents had to be content with the tours given by local boatmen and the frolic at the annual May picnic. By the late 1920s, this event had become key to state politics. It was a common boast that unless a candidate for governor announced his campaign at Wakulla Springs, he had no chance of winning the office. Unfortunately, the economic ravages of the Great Depression and increasingly rigid racial segregation soon combined to bring an end to this joyous — though sometimes partisan to the point of fisticuffs — gathering. In 1934, the picnic had declined to the point that "soft drinks and crackers constituted the only food offered for sale when noon-tide came, and the crowd thinned out noticeably."[18]

During the Depression, locals continued to long for the economic development of Wakulla Springs. In 1930, Christie announced his ultimate goal: to turn Wakulla Springs into "a wonderful tourist attraction similar to Silver Springs in Marion County." He promised development in a "highly legitimate manner," crushing any hopes for speakeasies or gambling dens at Wakulla. Christie also pledged to continue the tradition of public access to the spring for picnicking and swimming.[19] A year later, the Tallahassee newspaper was reminding its readers, "Wakulla Springs can be as valuable to Tallahassee as Silver Springs is to Ocala. As a business proposition it means much to Tallahassee merchants. In time Wakulla Springs will mean thousands and thousands of dollars to Tallahassee. How long depends on our boosting." That boosting was accomplished not only through breathless journalism, but also through Christie's herculean efforts to gain other types of publicity for Wakulla.[20]

Christie was a dedicated publicist, eager to take advantage of every type of mass media. In 1930, while clearing a swimming area, Christie's employees uncovered a number of mastodon bones. A team of scientists from the Florida Geological Survey worked to recover more specimens, and a trio of Pathe news cameramen captured a recreation of their underwater archeology. The first motion picture filmed at Wakulla Springs, it was made possible by the use of a glass diving bell, and it demonstrated the spring's incredible clarity to the nation. A second newsreel in 1931 covered the scenes along the river. Christie encouraged crowds to come and watch the filming of the archaeological project, and sent the marvelous mastodon bones on a state tour.[21]

During Christie's ownership, glass-bottom boats were introduced to Wakulla Springs. Christie courted every opportunity to send famous visitors across the spring in his new fleet. In 1933, he hosted the "Capital to Capital" motorcade, which included such dignitaries as Georgia's First Lady, Atlanta's mayor, and the president of the Coca-Cola Company. Christie welcomed Yasha Davidoff, a famous Russian singer, who expressed his appreciation for Wakulla's wonders by serenading the fish with his rendition of the "Volga Boatman." Even a group of Liberty County fiddlers made an appearance at the spring and composed a tune called "Moonlight on the Wakulla" to commemorate their visit.[22]

Despite his determined publicity, Christie joined the ranks of owners who failed to develop Wakulla Springs. A. L. Porter, Special Master in Chancery, put Christie's property up for public sale on May 7, 1934. The title went to F. G. Byrd of Leon County, who was acting on behalf of William Blount and Associates, also of Leon County. The price was $52,000.[23]

What would become of the "old fountain" now? Most residents probably assumed that Wakulla Springs would lapse into another period of neglect. Instead, the property had caught the eye of an important force in Florida real estate, a man quite capable of turning even the most unlikely tract into a thriving enterprise.

The date of Edward (Ed) Ball's first visit to Wakulla Springs is unknown. He most likely visited the area in the 1920s, when he was purchasing Florida acreage for his brother-in-law, Alfred I. DuPont. These tracts would eventually become the property of the St. Joe Paper Company. Ball also bought land for himself, and in June 1934 one of his companies, dubbed Wakulla Springs, Incorporated, began purchasing land around the site with the goal of acquiring the Wakulla Spring. Though a similarly named company — the Wakulla Springs Development Company — had purchased Christie's property from Byrd and his associates, Ball's firm won the mad scramble for river frontage. In September 1934, Ball bought the Wakulla Springs Development Company's acreage. Scooping up more land from African American turpentine workers, Ball built his Wakulla Springs, Incorporated holdings to 4,000 acres along two miles of the Wakulla River from its source at the spring.[24]

A new era, of both development and controversy, was about to begin.

A celebration at Wakulla Springs, circa 1900.
(State Archives of Florida)

Ed Ball opened the Wakulla Springs Lodge in September 1937.
(State Archives of Florida)

CHAPTER 4:
A Few Nickels and Dimes

In the middle of the Great Depression, Wakulla Springs became the property of a multimillionaire. Ed Ball could have cut off all access to the spring and the river's headwaters. He could have built a mansion or private hunting lodge. Instead, the quirky tycoon built a hotel and turned Wakulla Springs into a modest tourist attraction. While visitors were pleased with the long-awaited arrival of facilities at Wakulla, by the 1970s Ball's stewardship of Wakulla generated controversy, and legal battles erupted between parties who loved Wakulla Springs with equal intensity.

. . . .

Ed Ball's family traced its lineage to colonial Virginia and celebrated its connection to Mary Ball Washington, the mother of the nation's first president. Ball's father, Thomas Ball, served as a captain in the Confederacy and as a state senator in Texas before returning to his native Virginia with his wife, Lalla Gresham. The couple settled at Ball's Neck, where Ed, the youngest of five surviving children, was born on March 21, 1888. As a boy, Ball often skipped school, preferring to hunt and fish instead of studying. Alfred I. duPont, a scion of the great industrial clan, was a frequent visitor to the area, and Ball often served as his guide. The youth impressed duPont with his knowledge of nature as well as his skill with a gun.

Ball's family moved to Los Angeles in 1908, and Ball flitted from job to job, acquiring a practical business education in the process. He served in the U.S. Army from 1916 to 1919, though his unit never left the states during World War I. In 1920, Ed Ball's life changed when Alfred I. duPont wed Ball's older sister Jessie. The new Mrs. duPont urged her husband to take Ball on as a business partner, and this act of nepotism quickly paid dividends.[1]

Whatever Ed Ball lacked in formal schooling he made up for in shrewdness, loyalty, and natural financial acumen. Ball was instrumental in luring duPont to Florida, where Ball was engaged in buying up the wreckage of the Old South for the distinctly New South business of timber processing. While duPont was a dreamer, hoping to improve the lives of the Florida "Crackers," Ball was the realist who won business concessions from the state government and built the Florida National Bank chain.[2]

DuPont died in 1935, leaving his widow and his brother-in-law as the central figures of a vast business trust. Ball was charged with keeping the duPont Trust profitable for his sister and for the host of charities supported by the Nemours Foundation. Ball held that the estate should constantly enlarge and increase its profits. This meant expansion and frequent clashes, most famously with the employees of the Florida East Coast Railway. Ball cultivated a "public be damned" image while working closely with the "Pork Chop Gang" of North Florida legislators who controlled the statehouse until the mid-1960s. Ball also famously feuded with Senator Claude Pepper.[3]

Despite his irascibility, Ball had a great fondness for his adopted state and was a firm believer in the power of its tourism industry. "There's nothing in the world like Florida," he told one interviewer, "and the more people travel the more convinced they will become of that fact."[4] At Wakulla Springs, Ball created his own vision of Florida tourism, one that he felt deftly combined exploitation with conservationism. Inevitably, his ideas clashed with those of locals who saw greed rather than good stirring the waters of Wakulla Springs.

Though Ball controlled a vast network of enterprises, he took personal interest in small ventures. If a business struck him as having potential, he would frequently make the owner an offer for it on the spot. Ball built an odd collection of gas stations, hotels, and even a concession stand near Mt. Vernon. Whatever he owned,

Ball was determined to have it work for him. He soon applied this principle, which he called "picking up a few nickels and dimes," to Wakulla Springs.[5]

In 1935, Ball announced plans for the construction of a hotel at Wakulla Springs. The project rapidly became a favorite hobby. The Tallahassee *Daily Democrat* informed readers that the hotel was to be completely modern. Cost of construction was rumored to exceed $75,000, and the spring was to be altered by the creation of a white sand beach and a concrete bulkhead.[6]

Many months of hard labor were required to build a hotel so far from an urban center. The construction foreman hired white contractors from Jacksonville and Thomasville, but local African Americans, who were paid $1.25 to $1.50 a day based on their skills, did the heavy lifting. Squatters on the property were evicted as the outer structures of the resort, including the power station, water tower, piers, dressing rooms, and a pavilion, were built. After months of heat, mosquitoes, and hard work, the Wakulla Springs Lodge was opened to the public in September 1937.[7]

Tourists could access the lodge via a new road from Tallahassee just completed by the Works Progress Administration (WPA). Within a year, the tiny resort was garnering lavish praise from Florida travelers and receiving stellar reviews in the guidebooks. The *Album of Florida and West Indies Hotels* described the lodge as quiet and simple, but elegantly furnished, a place with "scenic beauty as old as the stars" with "facilities as advanced as tomorrow." State reviewers, including DeWitt Lamb of Jacksonville's *Florida Times-Union*, gave the place their blessings. Lamb was especially pleased that the new hotel in no way detracted from the beauty of the spring and that "none of the former pleasures as a gathering place and play park have been removed. If anything, these have been multiplied by adding those comforts which the spring's location and former isolation seemed to have made necessary and desirable."[8]

Though praised by many, the Wakulla Springs Lodge was firmly entrenched in the racial hierarchy of the Deep South. Room reservations were for whites only; though African Americans were employed in many capacities, they could not be guests. A 1952 letter from the lodge manager to a potential guest affirmed that the lodge could not accommodate the man's black valet, but offered to "assist you in locating quarters for your servants, and they will in all probability stay with some of the employees of the Lodge at their farmhouses near Wakulla."[9]

Ball's new venture did not please everyone, especially Wakulla County residents who lost their favorite hunting and fishing spots to his new wildlife preserve. The boatmen who had been independent operators were now forced to become Ball's employees or quit their profession. However, the Wakulla Springs Lodge offered improved economic opportunities to many local people. Especially for African Americans, work at the lodge was an attractive alternative to labor in the fields or turpentine camps. The pay was regular and a degree of advancement was possible. Entire families worked for Ball, with positions passed down through the generations. Journalist Keith Thomas, who worked at the lodge as a teenager in the 1970s, referred to it as "one of the best jobs I ever had" because of the extended network of family and friends behind the scenes.[10]

Ball took immense pride in Wakulla Springs. By the 1940s, Wakulla's iconic aspects — including the glass bottom boats and jungle cruises — were in place. Ball shrewdly hired Newton Perry, the "human fish," to be the lodge's manager. Robust and amiable, Perry staged underwater stunts and helped lure Hollywood film-makers to Wakulla Springs.[11] During World War II, Wakulla showed its patriotic side, hosting officers' families from nearby Camp Gordon Johnston and serving as a "best bet" for GIs on a weekend leave. On February 23, 1943, the roof of the lodge caught fire and was destroyed, but no guests were injured. A visiting cameraman captured the incident. It was a mark of Ball's paradoxical personality that he delighted in dragging out this movie reel to show to special guests.[12]

Military visitors, movie appearances, and glowing reviews in guidebooks made Wakulla Springs popular, but it never received the national publicity of its rivals. Silver Springs, Weeki Wachee, and Cypress Gardens were clearly besting Wakulla Springs in the fame game. Ball was failing to realize a profit, despite his hawk-like eye on the books. Many locals wondered why Ball was refusing to enlarge the facilities at Wakulla. On learning that Rainbow Springs was expanding in 1955, the Crawfordville *Wakulla News* ran a headline "Why Can't This Be Done With Wakulla Springs," urging Ball and "his bunch" to "get on the ball and do something big with Wakulla Springs." A 1960 *Tallahassee Democrat* article agreed that with expansion Wakulla Springs could be "perhaps Florida's top sight-seeing and recreational attraction north of the Gold Coast."[13]

Ball refused to budge. He enjoyed the park the way it was and loved using the lodge as a private retreat and a showplace for visiting dignitaries. Ball was fond of matching wits with his river guides, testing which of them could identify the most birds or spot the most alligators. He liked the southern cooking at the lodge and kept poultry on-site because he had an aversion to frozen meat. Ball maintained several residences, including a hotel suite in Jacksonville and a plantation in Leon County, but Wakulla clearly held special significance to him. His favorite time to stay was in the spring, when the dogwoods created the magical effect he called "Wakulla in white."[14] Ball's personal wealth and pleasure in Wakulla Springs meant he had no real need for expansion or profit. In 1974, Ball mused that Dick Pope, the impresario behind Cypress Gardens, "said that I was the only person he had ever met who was sitting on a fortune and wouldn't do anything with it, referring to the fact that I wasn't trying to turn Wakulla Springs into a honky-tonk."[15]

The first serious challenge to Ball's use of Wakulla Springs came from people reacting to the changes that Ball instituted in the late 1960s in order to increase the size of his tour boats and improve conditions for his workers. In 1969, after Ball had a new dock and ticket office built, and a chain link fence run between the lawn and the swimming beach (to prevent alligators and other animals from wandering onto the hotel grounds), the Audubon Society withdrew its sponsorship of Wakulla Springs as a bird sanctuary. A short time later, Ball squabbled with Wakulla County officials over a road that ran through his property, which he wanted to keep closed to outsiders. Ball uncharacteristically lost the case.[16] But the biggest conflict was in the works, and it focused on a fence.

Sometime in the 1960s, Ball had a chain-link fence installed across the Wakulla River approximately two miles downstream from the Wakulla Spring. Ball claimed the fence was necessary to prevent canoeists and motorboat operators from ascending the river and polluting his park. By Ball's logic, since he owned the land on both sides of the river, he owned the river bottom as well and thus was within his rights to fence it off and protect his property.

In 1971, locals began to question this assumption. If the Wakulla River was navigable, they argued, then Ball's fence across it was illegal. Thomas A. Morrill, a writer and former science teacher, and Jack Rudloe, an aquatics specimen collector from Panacea, filed a complaint to have the Wakulla River declared navigable to its source. The suit also claimed that Ball was damaging the ecosystem by dredging in the river and removing vital vegetation.[17]

The suit marked the first salvo in the long and complicated river war that Ball fought against the self-proclaimed environmentalists. What seemed to be truly at stake was not a fence but whether Ball planned further commercial development for Wakulla Springs. After decades of urging Ball to "do something" with Wakulla, many citizens now realized the danger inherent in tourism's exploitation of natural resources. They no longer trusted Ball not to build a honky-tonk.

Stymied by the courts, Morrill and Rudloe took their case to the public, and blatantly accused the state government of bending to Ball's will. In 1972, the Army Corps of Engineers declared the Wakulla River navigable to its source. Yet the fence remained as the conflict over it generated heated debate in the local newspapers. While many North Floridians were angered by the apparent arrogance of a rich man, others were equally disgusted that conservationists were fighting to open a pristine part of the river to sportsmen and polluters. In a surprising twist, a judge ruled that Ball's part of the river was not navigable and, chillingly, "owners have the legal right to impair or destroy the natural beauty of a river by acts committed on their own property lying above the mean high water line." After a series of appeals, lawyers on both sides decided it was unwise to continue the case and perhaps set a dangerous precedent for the freedom of landowners to destroy what were once considered sovereign waters.[18]

Though Ball's control of the Wakulla River was assured, two more incidents reflected conservationists' distrust of his motives and Ball's determination to keep Wakulla Springs his personal domain. Ball decided to place a massive cage on the banks of the river, extending out into the water, for the comfort of an aging black bear that he had adopted. Morrill objected, arguing that such an installment would "mean the complete development of Wakulla Springs as a tourist attraction." Ball was forced to get a permit for the cage, and though Algae the black bear died before his "big playpen" was completed, another orphaned bear took his place. In 1979, ten canoeists, mainly Florida State University students, were arrested for trespassing after they evaded the fence and paddled onto Ball's property. Though Morrill hoped the young people would contest the charges and establish a test case, the students were relieved to be sentenced to a day of picking up trash along the Wakulla River.[19]

Ed Ball never admitted to having any further plans for expansion or commercialization of Wakulla Springs. In his final years, Ball continued to visit Wakulla regularly, feeding his bear by hand and proudly pointing out "the most publicized fence in the world" to his guests. Former employee John Harvey, who worked at Wakulla Springs for thirty-five years, summed up Ball's fierce determination to protect his slice of paradise. "Mr. Ball loved Wakulla Springs. It was the apple of his eye. He would have fought anybody, forever, to keep them the way he wanted them."[20]

Ed Ball died on June 24, 1981, at the Ochsner Foundation hospital in New Orleans. The man fond of wishing "confusion to the enemy" in his nightly toasts had carefully left his affairs in order. Wakulla Springs passed into the hands of the Nemours Foundation, and lodge manager Joe Wilkie assured locals that no changes were planned for the park.[21]

Such was a fond but impossible hope. The ownership of Wakulla Springs would soon change dramatically, but controversies over its usage and preservation would continue.

Workers at Wakulla Spring at the waterfront in the late 1930s. (Wakulla Springs State Park)

World War II simulated combat training. Soldiers from Camp Gordon Johnston participated in propaganda movies shot at the spring. (Wakulla Springs State Park)

One of Florida's most powerful businessmen, Ed Ball considered
Wakulla Springs a prized possession and was determined to retain
total control over it. (State Archives of Florida)

A postcard from the 1950s highlights
Wakulla Springs swimming area and lodge.

The Wakulla River fence provoked a long-running court battle between
Ed Ball and local environmentalists. (Wakulla Springs State Park)

CHAPTER 5:
A Unique Resource

Upon Ed Ball's death, his Wakulla Springs property passed to the Nemours Foundation, a charitable organization that provided medical care for the elderly and for crippled children in Delaware and Florida, the states where Alfred I. duPont, the foundation's original benefactor, had spent much of his life. Five years later, it was apparent that Wakulla Springs, which had never made a profit for Ball, would not make money for Nemours. Despite a plethora of events such as folk festivals and rallies, in April 1985, the Nemours trustees announced that at least 3,000 acres of the Wakulla Springs property would be sold.[1] Suddenly, Wakulla Springs faced its greatest peril. Would it remain a low-key tourist attraction or become just another overdeveloped eyesore on the Florida scene?

· · · · · · · ·

During Ball's long running conflict over the Wakulla River fence, rumors hinted that state officials were unwilling to offend Ball because Ball was planning to donate Wakulla Springs to the people of Florida. Though such generosity failed to materialize, the idea that Wakulla Springs should be acquired by the state gained popularity. The ever-opinionated *Tallahassee Democrat* editorialized that it would be a shame to let Wakulla Springs "go condo." Instead, the state should buy the resort and allow it to remain an example of the "low-key, Big Bend brand of tourism."[2]

Nemours agreed to negotiate with the state before considering other offers. The State Conservation and Recreation Lands

Committee (CARL) ranked Wakulla Spring eleventh on its list of sixty-four properties proposed for state ownership. Wakulla Springs was unofficially valued at $7.5 million. James MacFarland, Director of the Division of State Lands, explained Wakulla's leapfrogging to nearly the top of the priority list: "It's a unique resource. Everybody thinks we have to have it."[3]

Some local resistance surfaced. Wakulla County Commissioner James Taylor estimated that the transfer of Wakulla Springs to the state would cost the county $30,000 a year in lost property taxes. This would be a significant blow to an economically depressed county where almost one-third of the land was already state-owned and therefore tax exempt. "I don't think we can stand anymore," Taylor argued, but the four-to-one County Commission vote in opposition to the state's purchase had no impact on the bargaining.[4]

Despite Florida's reputation for extended and frequently stalled negotiations, the Wakulla deal was pushed through in record time. A purchase agreement for $7.15 million was signed on May 21, 1986. In June, Governor Bob Graham and his Cabinet approved a plan for the future operation of Wakulla Springs. The purchase formally closed on September 30. On October 1, 1986, the historic attraction officially joined the state park system. Its legendary owner survived in the park's name: the Edward Ball Wakulla Springs State Park.[5]

The turnover made for immediate changes, despite the reassurances that Wakulla Springs would remain "just the way it is." The lodge and restaurant were under the auspices of the Florida State University Center for Professional Development, and the grounds and boats were now operated by the Florida Department of Natural Resources. Freedom, the last resident black bear, was relocated and his cage dismantled. The ban on alcohol in the lodge was lifted. Boat guides became more scientific and less folksy. A century-old tradition of free access to the grounds fell when admittance charges were added to the park.[6] The state's initial year of operation was marred on July 13, 1987 by the tragic death of Florida State University student George P. Cummings III, who was attacked and killed by an alligator. It was the first recorded alligator attack in Wakulla's history, and it occurred while the young man was snorkeling in the river, outside of the monitored swimming area. Much better publicity for the park arrived later that year, when the Wakulla Springs Dive Project set underwater endurance records and completed a number of revolutionary experiments in the spring.[7]

The state would soon learn, as Ed Ball had, that protecting Wakulla Springs was a full-time and often controversial occupation. Promoting tourism at the springs also brought the threat of development just beyond their gates, when individuals attempted to take advantage of proximity. Because of the fragile nature of the environment, even cautious development just outside of the park could endanger the aquifer and thus Wakulla Springs's celebrated water clarity. The battle between a citizen's right to profit and the state's mandate to protect dominated Wakulla's headlines for the last decade of the twentieth century.

In April 1993, Wakulla County real estate developer Ken Kirton purchased 63 acres of land, which included a swampy area and a sinkhole, at the northwest intersection of state roads 61 and 267, on the opposite corner from the state park. Kirton was soon asking the Board of Commissioners of Wakulla County to rezone his property from agricultural to commercial. Though he initially denied it was his intention, most people read into his actions the possibility of a gas station and convenience store on the property. While some residents welcomed the idea of a small business to provide services to park visitors, others were alarmed by the idea of spilled gas seeping through the aquifer and polluting the spring. Citizens pressured the commission, which had initially granted Kirton's request, to rescind it.[8]

Kirton was infuriated. A wiry, outspoken individual, he quickly became a folk hero to some and an anathema to others. He accused the commission of having a "vendetta" against him. In February 1994, he submitted another zoning request, this time from agricultural to commercial travel trailer park (CTTP). This would allow him to build a convenience store and a trailer park for recreational vehicles (RVs). Kirton vigorously argued that his business would meet a need, as the park lacked any facilities for campers. Fearful that this enterprise would cause traffic problems and be inconsistent with county planning, the commission denied Kirton's request on March 21. Kirton stormed out, vowing to keep fighting and to take his case to court.[9]

A public hearing on April 17, 1995, found Jim Stevenson of the Florida Department of Environmental Protection (DEP) expressing concern over the inevitable residue of any trailer park, including the dispensing of gasoline, the disposal of "gray water" from campers, and sewerage spills. "The cave system is immediately beneath the applicant's property," Stevenson argued. "There's no shortage of gas stations in Wakulla County. There is only one Wakulla Spring." However, as Kirton had agreed to a number of court-ordered stipulations on signage and waste storage, the commissioners told reporters they felt there would be no grounds for denying Kirton's request. The May 1 meeting proved fractious, with crowds carrying signs that read "SOS: Save Our Springs." Arguing that a potential legal battle with Kirton would be costly, and with Commissioner Angie Chappell, Kirton's most determined opponent, absent, the commissioners voted three to one to approve the rezoning.[10]

Other parties refused to yield. The Florida Wildlife Federation (FWF) brought suit against the Wakulla Board of Commissioners and Ken Kirton, charging that the rezoning violated the Wakulla County Comprehensive Plan of 1992, which called for the preservation of Wakulla Springs, as well as the Wakulla Spring Water Quality Protection Regulation Ordinance. Many hoped that Kirton's land would be purchased by the state or by the Apalachee Land Conservancy (ALC), thus protecting the springs and solving the problem.[11]

In August, an ALC worker spotted heavy vehicles clearing Kirton's property. Questioned, Kirton announced that any deal for his land was off and that he intended to build "Kirton's Korner," a 6,000 square foot welcome station/store with an RV park attached. While Kirton told news reporters that he had no plans to dispense gasoline, Commissioner Chappell accused him of lying, referencing private communications in which Kirton had said that the only way to make money on the spot was to sell gas. On October 17, Judge

Phil Padovano issued an injunction to halt construction until the conflict was resolved.[12]

With each setback, Kirton's plans grew more elaborate. In December 1995, he announced that he would build a bed and breakfast inn and a stable on a second tract he owned near the park, dubbing this enterprise 'Kirton's Kurve.' He would later claim to be in favor of establishing a low-impact, primitive campground with the slogan "Kountree Kampin located at Kirton's Korner. Wakulla Springs is located next to us." His public behavior grew ever more erratic, including handing out white flowers at county commission meetings and creating hideous "art" made of bleach jugs, feed sacks, cow bones, and car parts, which he displayed at his "korner."[13]

Two long years of delays and legal snarls meant the case played out as much in the media as in the courtroom. On May 23, 1997, Circuit Judge Royce Agner finally found in favor of the FWF. The Kirton property would be zoned agricultural, preventing him from building on the tract. The decision was appealed, but the First District Court of Appeal upheld it in early 1998.[14]

Determined to end the fight and save Wakulla Springs, Florida's attorney general filed an eminent domain claim in 1999. As negotiations began, Kirton announced yet another spectacular scheme for his land, clearly a move to try and raise its fair price. Kirton proclaimed that he could built a rodeo arena, tourist cottages, an equestrian center, a conference center, tennis courts, and four retail shops, along with his previously planned convenience store, RV park, and campground. The state offered $400,000 for the land. Kirton demanded close to $1,000,000. Talks broke down and Kirton's case went back to the court, this time in search of a price tag.[15]

On July 19, 1999, the state cut Kirton a check for $450,000. Kirton's Wakulla properties were combined into Wakulla Springs. "This is a huge step forward in the protection of the Edward Ball Wakulla Springs State Park," DEP Director Fran Mainella announced. "We are grateful to everyone who worked so hard to protect one of Florida's natural systems."[16] Kirton's case ended in 2000, when he was awarded a total of $650,000 for his land, as well as court costs, attorneys' fees, and $16,000 in interest that had accrued since the state condemned his property. "The state gave me the doubt of the benefit and the jury gave me the benefit of the doubt," Kirton said.[17]

The battle over Kirton's Korner provoked harsh words and hard feelings on both sides of the issue, as well as the highway. Many Wakulla County residents were angered that the state promoted tourism as a viable industry but refused to allow an individual to profit from land he owned in enviable proximity to a park. Others felt that any business close to Wakulla Springs was a risk factor to the environment. And some argued that whether the enterprise was a neon-lit gas station or an environmentally friendly campground, it would set an unfortunate precedent. Heavy traffic, noise, pollution, and general unsightliness are common on long stretches of highway in Central and South Florida. By preventing it from taking root near Wakulla Springs, residents of the Big Bend had made a statement about their quality of life.

A sign at the disputed property expressed both Ken Kirton's intentions and his opponents' eventual victory over them. (B. R. Black)

Lodge entrance. (Wakulla Springs State Park)

Views through the glass used to let visitors see the crystal clear bottom of the spring. (State Archives of Florida)

Youngsters enjoying the diving platform over the spring basin. (State Archives of Florida)

Members of the Tarpon Club, the synchronized swimming team of Florida State College for Women (now FSU) were sometimes featured in movies filmed at the spring. (State Archives of Florida)

CHAPTER 6:
Myth and Magic

Wakulla Springs has inspired many legends, stories, poems, tall tales, and novels. Though most of the literature is obscure, its imagery is rich and vivid. In the twentieth century new forms of media worked to make Wakulla Springs immortal. Collectively, these artistic endeavors reflect Wakulla's continuing fascination and novelty.

· · · · · · · ·

Ponce de Leon's quest for the fountain of youth is Florida's foundational legend. For generations, schoolchildren were taught that the aged conquistador discovered Florida while questing for a supernatural spring that would make him young again. There is no historical evidence to support this claim, and the story appears to be a nineteenth-century romantic invention. Though false, the tale remains delightful, and Victorian visitors to Wakulla Springs can be forgiven for how readily they imagined the conquistador's reflection in their local waters.[1]

Many early Wakulla stories claim to be based on Native American legends. Whatever tales the Timucuan and Apalachee told have been lost to time. While some nineteenth century visitors may have heard the oral traditions of the Creek and Seminole tribes, the stories that appeared in books and newspapers were echoes of what Americans thought an "old Indian tale" should sound like. One dubious myth claims that after Toltec priests fled Mexico in the wake of an Aztec invasion, they ceremoniously lowered their golden idols into the Wakulla Spring, which they believed was the sanctum of a stronger god. "Toltecs will be free from Aztec rule when the Waters of Wakulla wash our gods to the sea," the high priest proclaimed. This fanciful fable sought to explain the flecks of gold that occasionally twinkled on the bottom of the spring.[2]

Another tale with a slightly stronger claim to Indian folklore was related in 1856 by Charles Lanman, who claimed to have heard it from "ancient Seminoles." They informed him that fairy creatures regularly danced in the spring's waters, except on the night of the full moon, when a "gigantic warrior, sitting in a stone canoe, with a copper paddle in his hand," frightened them away.[3]

In sharp contrast to manufactured myths was the true story of Milly Francis, Florida's own Pocahontas. During Andrew Jackson's 1818 incursion, Duncan McKrimmon, a young militiaman from Georgia, was captured by Creek braves and taken to Francis Town, on the banks of the Wakulla River. Milly Francis was the fifteen-year-old daughter of Chief Hillis Hadjo (also known as Francis the Prophet), and when she saw that the soldier was to be executed, she begged for his life, arguing that he was too young to have gone to war on his own accord and should not be punished for what his elders had forced him to do. Her eloquence won the day. Many years later, an American army officer familiar with the tale located Milly Francis in exile in Arkansas, and lobbied for her courage to be recognized. Congress granted her a small pension and a medal, but these belated rewards reached her on her deathbed.[4]

Natural oddities, especially the massive mastodon bones that rest on the spring floor, have inspired many humorous stories to explain their presence. In 1850, Professor George S. King blamed the mastodon's "Indian rider" for steering his steed into the spring. In 1873, a satiric newspaper article claimed that recent discoveries in Spanish archives had finally revealed the truth — the bones were those of the pet elephant kept by Ponce de Leon's lover, the exotic princess "Lalla-minx." Anxious to bathe in the fountain of youth (which, naturally, was the Wakulla Spring), the princess tragically lost control of her elephant. The unfortunate creature perished with Lalla-minx still aboard his back. The writer of the article hoped that one day the bones of the "petrified princess" might be found in the

Wakulla basin.[5]

Another oddity that inspired legends is the Wakulla smoke, also known as the Wakulla volcano. Early settlers in Tallahassee often noticed a cloud of smoke rising from the southern swamps, and believed that it marked an Indian camp or pirate's hideout. In the 1880s, a number of gentleman adventurers sought the source of the cloud. They found little more than rocks and rattlesnakes, but the tale of a "volcano" that can never be found is sometimes related to gullible tourists who spot strange clouds over the landscape.[6]

Wakulla Springs has served as a backdrop for several novels. Kirk Munroe, an imitator of Horatio Alger, produced a steady stream of novels of the "rags to riches" genre. Munroe set many of his adventures in Florida, including *Big Cypress* and *The Flamingo Feather*. *Wakulla*, published in 1886, told the story of a family that moves from Maine to Florida to rebuild an old plantation. Wakulla is actually the name of the town, which was modeled on Newport. The young hero has a number of mishaps in the wild, including being washed through a sinkhole into a spring.[7] Wakulla was also mentioned in Mary Bethel Alfriend's historical novels, which focused on Spanish colonial life around Tallahassee. In *Juan Ortiz: Gentleman of Seville* (1940), Spanish soldiers and a priest travel to the Wakulla Spring, where the priest marvels at God's creation while the soldiers take a much-needed bath.[8]

More recent books featuring Wakulla Springs include Nanci Kincaid's *Crossing Blood* (1993), a period piece set in Tallahassee during the Civil Rights Movement. For the novel's protagonist, a young child, Wakulla Springs is a refuge from the increasingly troubled city, a place that "was cold no matter how hot the world was." *Smiling Jack Yeager*, an autobiography, recounts the author's days as an underwater film star and stunt double for Tarzan. Perhaps inspired in part by these local memories, Russ Franklin entitled his 1999 novella *Strong Like Johnny Weissmuller*, and gave his main character a father who, like Yeager, had been a stand-in for the Lord of the Apes.[9] M.D. Abrams's novel *Murder at Wakulla Springs* (2006) provides local color and environmental information along with a killing investigated by an actress and a detective. Four generations of an African American family share a mystical experience in Andy Duncan and Ellen Klages's *Wakulla Springs*, which won the 2014 World Fantasy Award for best novella.[10]

Wakulla Springs inspires poetry at almost the speed it churns out water. The spring was the favored subject of vast amounts of Victorian doggerel. Many of these poems mimicked Longfellow's "Hiawatha" and attempted to create Native American myths, with very little success. "Wachulla," published by Kate A. DuBose in 1849, went on for 117 lines, meandering through Indian imagery, descriptions of nature, and philosophical musing. Perhaps the most ambitious of these poems was "Legend of Wakulla" by Reinette Gamble Long. Published in a 1922 collection, the poem utilized the Wakulla volcano as well as the spring, telling the story of the lovers Osola and Wannawachee. Osola, a noble warrior, refuses to run away with the beautiful maiden Wannawachee because he must keep a signal fire burning for his father, who has travelled to a distant council meeting. Tragically, the pair is lured to the spirit world beneath the river by jealous fairies, though they emerge each night to light the flaming beacon.[11]

Modern poetry about Wakulla is less structured and more focused on imagery. *Wakulla Portraits: Poetry and Photography* (1983) is an eclectic collection that examines different aspects of the spring and river. Leon Stokesbury's "Wakulla Springs" pokes fun at the exaggerations of the boat guides and the bad behavior of the tourists. Other poems feature meditations on alligators, bass, and the cypress trees.[12]

Artists likewise have found inspiration at Wakulla. In 1960, Chicago artist Charles Balchunas developed a technique for painting underwater, in hopes of capturing the truest colors of the spring. Watercolorist Mary Jo Weale's works are scattered around the lodge, many of them hanging in guest rooms. Muralist Richard Hass created a series of Panhandle landmarks, including Wakulla Springs, in his work for an office complex in Tallahassee.[13] Undoubtedly many handmade sketches and photographic masterpieces have been made at Wakulla and now reside in family albums.

Wakulla's greatest cultural fame comes from the movies

partially filmed on site. In an age before computer-generated imagery (CGI), any realistic underwater scenes in a motion picture required finding somewhere with perfect water clarity. Wakulla Springs was a "natural" at this type of performance. The Pathe newsreels made in 1931 established Wakulla as a place for a director who needed a unique location for his aquatic special effects.

In 1943, the Camp Gordon Johnston Amphibious Training Center staged a mock combat at Wakulla Springs for the Grantland Rice Sportlight camera. Over a dozen men demonstrated their martial skills with machine guns, automatic rifles, and dynamite. Bold recruits swam beneath a burning gasoline spill, and a dummy Japanese boat exploded as planes strafed the spring. The resulting short subject that featured "the toughest training in the army" won an Academy Award the following spring.[14]

Tarzan swung through Wakulla Springs in the 1940s. The films featuring Johnny Weissmuller were among the most popular movies of the era. *Tarzan's Secret Treasure* (1941) and *Tarzan's New York Adventure* (1942) included scenes filmed at the spring and along the river. Newton Perry, Ed Ball's lodge manager, was instrumental in bringing the Metro-Goldwyn-Mayer filmmakers to Wakulla and served as a stuntman, swimming coach, and casting director for extras. Many of the "primitive savages" who menaced Tarzan were Wakulla County schoolboys and farmers, and several local young women swam underwater, doubling for Jane. Much to his director's horror, Weissmuller had the diving platform above the spring raised to a perilous height for practice plunges. Weissmuller stayed at the lodge, where he enjoyed flirting with local girls and ordering his breakfast by sticking his head out of his window and bellowing his famous Tarzan yell.[15]

Perry also recruited good swimmers and bathing beauties for a series of novelty short subjects filmed in the 1940s. The films often featured members of the Tarpon Club, the synchronized swimming team of Florida State College for Women (now FSU). Perry's merry troupe performed water ballets and staged stunts like underwater picnics, where the kids ate food and "smoked" cigarettes, a trick accomplished by releasing a mouthful of milk with each "puff."

Perry left Wakulla Springs in 1944, transferring his talents to Weeki Wachee Springs, where he created the world-famous mermaid show.[16]

Wakulla's most memorable film feature involved a lovelorn monster. The Wakulla River doubled for the Amazon as a team of scientists and the requisite pretty girl went in search of the gillman, a missing link between humans and amphibians. The movie was essentially a retelling of the Beauty and the Beast fairy tale, with the addition of "moody underwater cinematography and claustrophobic moss-covered thrills." *The Creature From The Black Lagoon* (1954) was a 3-D hit and remains a Universal monster movie classic.

Rico Browning, a Tallahassee man who was working at Wakulla Springs, performed the amazing stunt work for the Creature. The filmmakers needed a strong swimmer to perform in test footage. Browning's unusual stroke caught the attention of director Jack Arnold, who immediately cast him as the Creature for the underwater shots. Browning helped design a sponge rubber suit that wouldn't drown him. The suit lacked room for air tanks, forcing him to breathe through an air hose while waiting underwater for his cue. Browning went on to perform in many movies and TV shows, but he always retained a special affection for the Creature. The success of the movie promoted two sequels, and some scenes of *The Creature Walks Among Us* (1956) were filmed at Wakulla.[17]

Another underwater epic to capitalize on Wakulla's water clarity was *Around the World Under the Sea* (1965). Directed by Andrew Marton, the film starred Lloyd Bridges, Shirley Eaton, Brian Kelly, and David McCallum as marine scientists who have perilous encounters with underwater volcanoes and giant eels. Heavy rains washed tannic acid into the spring, limiting the number of shots filmed, but locals marveled at a number of bizarre props brought in for the production, including a shell-shaped house and a dummy diver.[18]

Joe Panther, a 1976 family adventure, had a number of sequences filmed at Wakulla Springs. The selection of Wakulla as a location came via family connections; the author of the Joe Panther books had a brother who worked at the lodge. Described as "the

Hardy Boys as Native Americans," the film was the coming of age story of a boy in the Everglades, and starred Ray Tracey, Ricardo Montalban, and Brian Keith. Wakulla was used primarily for an underwater rescue sequence, with Rico Browning directing the action.[19]

A final major film to utilize Wakulla's waters was *Airport '77*. One in a long string of 1970s disaster movies, it told the story of a wealthy art collector whose private 747, packed with friends and precious paintings, crashes into the ocean. Jimmy Stewart starred as the billionaire, and one of his unfortunate passengers was Olivia de Haviland. Jack Lemmon starred as the heroic pilot.

A large crew worked at the spring through October and November 1976, struggling against bad weather to complete underwater effects which would account for only four to eight minutes of screen time. Delays cost the company $20,000 a day in salaries alone. The crew lowered a 70-foot mock-up of a 747's fuselage and wing into the spring, positioning it cautiously on the cavern ledge, while local divers assisted and made sure that no Hollywood types went sight-seeing in the cave. Jack Lemmon was the only star to be filmed at Wakulla, in a scene that required him to don a wetsuit and scuba gear and descend to the window of the plane, where he would wave at his rescuers. Lemmon spent most of his time in the Tallahassee Hilton, smoking cigars and working crossword puzzles as he waited for his shot to be readied. The jaunty actor revealed that this was "the hardest I've ever worked on a movie. I told them when we started, I'm a lover, not an athlete." Still, he gamely descended into the spring, and after a female alligator cruised near the set he quipped, "I hope she doesn't decide she wants to get into movies." Sadly, Wakulla Springs was not listed in the film's credits because the underwater shots were so brief and unidentifiable.[20]

Advances in movie technology, and the tragic darkening of the spring, make it unlikely that Wakulla will ever again answer Hollywood's call. However, television budgets are much more limited, and the park still can double for almost any swamp or jungle locale. In 1999, a film crew from Principal Films, Ltd., a London company, arrived to shoot scenes for a Discovery Channel show called *Break Out*. Two segments of the six-part series on famous escapes were filmed, with Wakulla Springs standing in for the Philippines and Vietnam. FSU film students and local woodsman George Weymouth had bit parts in the episodes.[21]

While Wakulla Springs's heyday as a film location may have ended in the 1970s, its Hollywood connection is celebrated on the boat tours and in the lodge, where movie posters conjure Tarzan and the Creature. Wakulla's contribution to film's golden age of adventure and suspense adds to the park's decidedly nostalgic appeal.

The diaster film *Airport '77* utilized Wakulla's waters, and starred Jack Lemmon as the heroic pilot who was "rescued" from a watery plane crash. Upon seeing a female alligator, he said, "I hope she doesn't decide she wants to get into movies." (Wakulla Springs State Park)

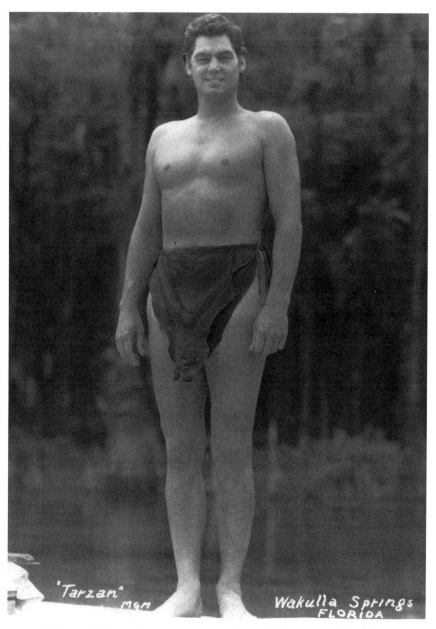

Johnny Weissmuller as Tarzan with Wakulla Springs doubling for a jungle in Africa. (Wakulla Srings State Park)

During his stay at Wakulla Springs, Johnny Weissmuller requested
an extra diving platform, from which he made spectacular leaps
for his movie stunts. (Wakulla Springs State Park)

Rico Browning's unusual swimming style won him the title role in *The Creature from the Black Lagoon*. (Wakulla Springs State Park)

Paleoindians camping near the spring more than 10,000 years ago used this large stone blade. State archaeologist Calvin Jones unearthed the lithic near the Wakulla lodge in 1995. (Wakulla Springs State Park)

CHAPTER 7:
The Joy of Discovery

For over three centuries, scientists have been fascinated by Wakulla Springs. From the gentleman naturalists at the twilight of the Enlightenment to the modern aquatic explorers using advanced computer technology to plunge into the very heart of the spring, as well as the intrepid archaeologists who seek man's prehistory in bones and stones, the search for answers has become a regular facet of the Wakulla scene.

. . . .

Wakulla Springs was unknown to Colonial and Revolutionary Era investigators. Andrew Ellicott, a celebrated American surveyor, made the first scientific observations of Wakulla in 1799. He wrote that the "Apalachy" River rose from a single limestone spring. During Andrew Jackson's invasion, Captain Hugh Young, a topographical engineer, drafted a valuable report that described the quality of the land along the river and the plants that clogged it, but declared the spring water to be "unhealthy." This report was probably never made public. Though not strictly a scientific observer, John Lee Williams described the Wakully River with its spring of unknown depth and its "squadrons of fish." This depiction, which appeared in two books by Williams, must have tweaked scientific curiosity among his readers.[1]

Francis de La Port, Comte de Castelnau, was the first trained scientist to visit Wakulla. Already famous as a naturalist and international traveler, Castelnau mustered twenty armed men and a number of boats for his February 18, 1838 ascent of the river.

It was a dangerous mission due to the deprivations of the Second Seminole War. Joseph Delafield, president of the Natural History Lyceum of New York and a general agent for the Apalachicola Land Company, accompanied the Frenchman. Castelnau carefully recorded the wide variety of plant and animal life, including the fifteen-foot-long alligators. Sounding the spring was a vexing task, and the members of the crew could not concur on its proper depth, but they agreed that its water was refreshing and pure. The men camped on the riverbank near a tree that bore the mark of Tiger Tail, a local Seminole warrior. Panther screams disturbed their sleep, and in the morning one man found a snake in his bedroll, but all the explorers returned to St. Marks safely. Castelnau published his findings in French scientific journals, along with the wry comment that Wakulla Springs "will be a wonderful haunt for the naturalist when he can pursue his investigation calmly without fear of savages emerging from the bushes to claim his scalp."[2]

By the 1850s, visitors to the spring were reporting something previous investigators had missed. Shifting sands on the spring basin or perhaps a better view from some type of crude glass-bottom boat now revealed a collection of huge, odd-shaped bones on the spring basin. Sarah A. Smith of Tallahassee correctly identified these relics as the remains of a mastodon.[3] In June 1850, Professor George S. King, a resident of Newport, along with an assistant constructed a special pair of tongs and "fished" for the bones in a manner that would make a modern paleontologist cringe. In one afternoon, the pair brought up leg bones, knee joints, vertebra, hip bones, and a tusk that immediately crumbled. These remarkable bones vanished when the ship carrying them to a northern museum was lost at sea. Fortunately, the Wakulla Springs property has proven to be a virtual graveyard of mastodons and other extinct animals. More bones were recovered in and around the spring in 1858, 1895, and 1902.[4]

In 1930, workers clearing a swimming area stumbled upon bones in relatively shallow water. The Florida Geological Survey took charge of the find. Divers in heavy helmets guided suction hoses to remove debris and then lifted the bones to the surface. Though still a primitive form of retrieval, the Survey's efforts freed a nearly complete mastodon skeleton, which now resides in the Museum of Florida History in Tallahassee.[5]

Ed Ball's purchase of Wakulla Springs meant it would be off-limits to independent researchers. The Wakulla Spring cave was tempting to anyone with a pair of fins and an air tank, but the tragic deaths of some young free divers, who perished while attempting to reach the cave ledge, led Ball to ban all diving in the spring.

Six FSU students were determined to find their way in, and used practice dives at Natural Bridge Sink to perfect their safety techniques. Gary Salsman and two friends volunteered to assist with some underwater filming and were granted the rare privilege of diving to the spring cave. They found and raised a mastodon bone from the cave's floor. Their discovery led to a lifting of the ban for sanctioned personnel.[6]

Over 200 accident-free dives were made by the students from 1955 to 1957. Working without wet suits, they made a series of gradual penetrations into the cave. The limits of technology and the risk of getting the bends forced the divers to keep their adventures inside the cave to under fifteen minutes in length. The young men discovered a "bone yard" on the cave floor. The apparent sorting of bone types, along with the presence of spear points, led to speculation that the Wakulla cave was once on dry land and sheltered prehistoric peoples. The team also discovered vast formations inside the cave, including a "Grand Canyon." When their explorations concluded in June 1957, the divers had reached a point 950 feet from the mouth of the cave at a depth of 240 feet.[7]

The period of sanctioned diving ended in 1961 due to concerns over liability after several swimming accidents and deaths at the spring. Well-trained divers were angered at this new ban. One sportswriter dubbed Wakulla Springs "the cradle of underwater sports on the North American continent," and while he conceded that Ball had every right to close the spring, he hoped "that in time he [Ball] will see that nothing is to be gained by denying his neighbors and fellow creatures the benefit of this awe-inspiring masterpiece of nature."[8]

The state's purchase of Wakulla Springs opened up new

possibilities for scientific research. In October 1986, the United States Deep Caving Team gained permission to use the spring. Team leader Dr. William Stone assembled an international cast of divers, crewmen, and scientists. Equipped with advanced technology, the team had three main objectives: explore and chart the Wakulla cave; test a new closed circuit life support apparatus called a rebreather; and conduct studies in the geology, hydrology, and biology of the spring. To increase dive time, the team built an underwater "habitat" which permitted up to 36 hours of decompression. Divers in the habitat could communicate with the surface via telephones and have meals from the lodge delivered to them in airtight containers. To speed their exploration, the divers rode self-propelled vehicles called sleds. These devices were playfully dubbed the "Starship Enterprise" and the "Klingon Kruiser." The National Geographic Society and numerous private and corporate sponsors underwrote this expensive and revolutionary project.[9]

The expedition was a six-week journey into "Wakulla's inner space." Twenty-three dives were made, and many were filmed. More than two miles of central tunnels were mapped at an average depth of 260 to 320 feet. Four side tunnels were also explored. Dive times ranged from 40 to 80 minutes, and the farthest penetration was made at 4,176 feet from the cave entrance at a depth of 360 feet.

The team accomplished its objectives, adding significantly to mankind's knowledge of the Wakulla Spring. Dye tracing and uranium isotope testing revealed underwater links between Indian Spring, Sally Ward Spring, and Wakulla. Blind albino catfish were collected and studied. The rebreather, which recycled breathable air to maximize a diver's time underwater, passed its most rigorous tests. When the project concluded on December 30, 1987, the "aquanauts" left behind an astounding amount of data and incredible footage of Wakulla's limestone labyrinths.[10]

The 1990s witnessed another period of underwater exploration, beginning with "guerilla" divers who slipped into Sally Ward Spring under cover of darkness. In October 1991, the Woodville Karst Plain Project (WKPP) began sanctioned work, building on the legacy of Salsman and Stone. Named for the 400 square mile layer of limestone that stretches from Tallahassee to the Gulf, this nonprofit organization of divers is dedicated to tracing the passages between springs and sinkholes to better understand the workings of Florida's water supply.[11]

Divers George Irvine, Jarrold Jablonski, and Brent Scarabin began setting and breaking records with yearly punctuality. In 1996, they pushed to 10,000 feet from the cave mouth. Using rebreathers, they posted a distance of 11,000 feet in 1997. With homemade sleds and decompression chambers shaped from cow troughs, kiddie pools, and scuba tanks, the intrepid trio made a 18,000 foot penetration in 1998. The divers added extensive details to the Wakulla map and discovered that one tunnel was probably linked to Spring Creek Springs. They also discovered a chamber dominated by a large rectangular stone, an echo of the iconic image from *2001: A Space Odyssey*. Diver Wes Stiles recalled that moment: "It seemed to me that, just like in the movie, we were exploring an alien world."[12]

The United States Deep Caving Team returned to Wakulla in 1998 with the ultimate goal of developing a three-dimensional map of the Wakulla system. This map would be vital to scientists and water management officials. A digital wall mapper (DWM) that emitted sonar pulses was mounted to an underwater scooter, with an onboard computer to record its data. Eleven people representing five countries participated in the project, which was frustratingly delayed by two hurricanes.

Dives lasted as long as four hours, requiring divers to spend up to thirteen hours in the habitat to decompress. The new habitat was placed on a barge, rather than underwater, and divers entered it through a tiny, perfectly pressured metal compartment. Stocked with clothes, books, a toilet and a DVD player, rangers joked that the habitat was "the only camping permitted at Wakulla Springs."[13]

The team ran 27 missions inside the Wakulla cave, creating a digital picture of the world below the lodge. Unfortunately, this knowledge came at a high price, as a volunteer diver was killed during one of the missions, due to his lack of experience with a rebreather.

In the summer of 2000, the WKPP volunteers returned to

their work, setting a 19,000 feet dive record and mapping caverns beneath the boat platforms. A drought meant that almost no tannic acid, which clouds water, had washed into the spring. These ideal conditions made it possible for divers to spot the "fossils and bones coming out of the walls" in the caverns. The WKPP team theorized that Wakulla Springs was linked to numerous other cave systems and their testimony was essential in making the case against Ken Kirton's proposed development of nearby land.[14]

Wakulla's mysteries inspire digging as well as diving. In 1998, the Florida Bureau of Archaeological Research accessed potential archaeological sites on the property. Though only a preliminary step, the summer of investigation revealed the rich history of human usage of the property. Stephen Bryne and Thomas Kempton's fieldwork identified 54 archaeological or historic sites. Even without extensive excavation, the pair found stone tools and broken ceramics from the Indian periods, as well as hotel china, turpentine buckets, and whiskey bottles.[15]

One of the most promising sites was 8WA321, a cleared three acre field on the south bank of the river approximately 1/3 of a mile east of the lodge. Known to park rangers as the "Bear Site," it had formerly been the home of Ed Ball's orphaned bears. In 1992, Calvin Jones of the Bureau of Archaeological Research led an excavation of this site. Dubbed "the people's archaeologist" for his ease in explaining complicated finds, Jones led a team of rangers and volunteers in a torturous July dig. Battling heat, ticks, and swarming insects, they opened 31 test pits at the site.

The dig results were amazing: 1224 artifacts from four distinct periods of cultural development, including shards of Spanish olive jars, were taken from the earth. The cluster of materials might indicate the spot was a landing place for canoes. Its proximity to an Indian mound of the Weeden Island period also raises the possibility that the site was a settled village or religious center. The site might well be the location of Aute, the Indian village sought by de Soto. If this speculation is someday confirmed by further discoveries, according to Jones, Wakulla Springs would become "the oldest known or identified actual site visited by Europeans in the mainland of the United States."[16]

Site 8WA329 might also hold important artifacts. The sandy ridge crest now occupied by the lodge seems a likely place for people of the Paleoindian and Early Archaic periods to have camped. When a sewer line replacement necessitated digging around the lodge in 1994, Jones and his helpers were quick to investigate the project impact areas.

The new route was systematically sampled. The team conducted excavations in 48 sites. Artifacts from virtually every era were discovered. A number of Early Archaic projectile points/ knife types known as Bolen Beveled points were uncovered, but no human remains or burial sites were identified.

Perhaps the most exciting moment in Wakulla's archaeological history came on January 23, 1995, when Jones unearthed a large bifacial tool in a trench near the gift shop entrance to the lodge. Made of local chert and shaped in a style known as the Simpson point, the blade measured 7 ¼ inches long and 4 inches wide. It would have been used by First Floridians to separate hides from large animals.

Jones's maxim was "if you listen real close, the ground will talk to you." Finding such a large, precious blade and other tools allowed archaeologists to offer a further hypothesis on how so many animal bones might have arrived in and around the Wakulla cave. With sea levels dramatically lower some 10,000 years in the past, the Wakulla cave was on dry land, though it may have contained a spring as a water source. Natives camped high on the ridge, so they would not startle their prey, which came to drink in the cave. By hiding along the cave ledge, Indians could have sprung their traps as animals entered or exited the cave, and then dragged the carcasses to the higher ridge for processing. Jones offered a delightful scenario: the mastodon standing in the Museum of Florida History might have been skinned with the Simpson point he recovered from the ground.[17]

Jones died on February 15, 1998, but his amazing find is honored in an interpretative exhibit beside the lodge. The display holds a replica of the blade. Labeled "A Point in Prehistory," it also shows Jones standing in the trench, holding up the remarkable artifact.[18]

Wakulla Springs has always fascinated curious minds. With so many mysteries and secrets, for over two centuries it has welcomed naturalists, chemists, biologists, and archaeologists. Amateurs as well as the professionally trained have conducted studies along its banks. But with the dawn of the twenty-first century, science at Wakulla took on a new urgency, as mysterious and deadly forces threatened the great spring and its river. These mysteries must be solved if Wakulla Springs is to endure.

The Wakulla mastodon as displayed at the Museum of Florida History in Tallahassee. (Museum of Florida History)

Dr. Herman Gunter, shown holding a mastodon tusk, and colleagues from the Florida Geological Survey raised and assembled the nearly complete mastodon skeleton discovered in the Wakulla Spring. (Wakulla Springs State Park)

Mastodon and other bones remain inside the cave opening. (Wakulla Springs State Park)

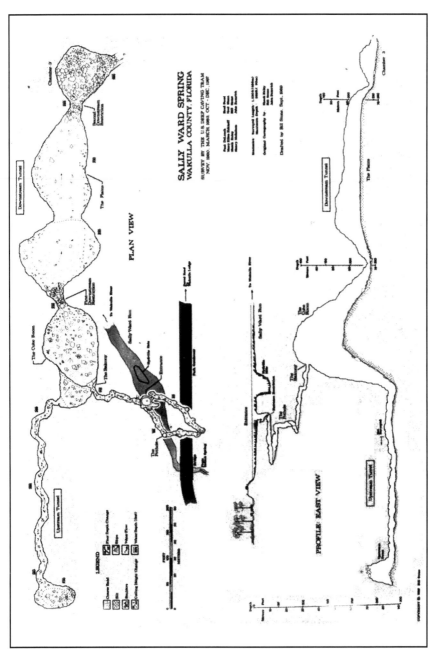

The 1987 map illustrates the underwater labyrinth of the Wakulla cave beneath Sally Ward Spring. (U.S Deep Caving Team)

A member of Gary Salsman's team descends during the initial cave diving explorations in the 1950s. (Wakulla Springs State Park)

Young supporters of the preservation efforts of Wakulla
Springs. (Wakulla Springs State Park)

CHAPTER 8:
Darker Waters

A s the twentieth century drew to a close, the Edward Ball Wakulla Springs State Park seemed relatively unchanged from its days as a millionaire's beloved attraction. Yet within and beneath the park, major alterations were occurring. Some were due to shifts in management style and the addition of new properties. Others were literally darker and more invasive, ominous shadows that tainted the spring's legendary clarity and signaled an ecological system in peril.

· · · · · · · ·

Wakulla Springs had quickly proven to be an expensive property to maintain. In November 1994, the management of the park was consolidated under the auspices of the Florida Park Service. Many of the environmental and maintenance problems the park faced predated its purchase by the state. Construction of a new sewage collection and treatment operation replaced the two outdated septic tanks that had served the property. This state-of-the-art system was designed to respect the Wakulla Springs Protection Zone and prevent groundwater contamination. Further renovation to the lodge lobby was made that same year, thanks to a funding gift from the St. Joe Paper Company. The lobby was refurbished to its 1937 appearance, and improvements were made to the dining area, which was renamed the Ball Room. An even more extensive "face-lift" was performed in 1996, when the lodge was closed section by section for repairs to the kitchen, guest rooms, and exterior. The project cost $820,000. At a ceremony celebrating the completion of the project, Fran P. Mainella, Director of the Department of Environmental Protection's Division of Recreation and Parks, summed up the renovation's intent: "The greatest compliment our guests at Wakulla Springs pay us is to say that over the years, it has not changed."[1]

Along with repairing the lodge, the Florida Park Service confronted the problems of new additions to the property. Of the 3,251 acres added in 1999, the most problematic was Cherokee Sink, a sinkhole with historical and hydrological connections to the Wakulla Spring. The sink had long been a popular swimming hole for the community, and in the 1960s it became notorious as a party spot. When asked why he didn't put a stop to the dope-smoking and beer-drinking shenanigans at Cherokee Sink (which he also owned), Ed Ball supposedly replied, "Let them go over there. That'll keep 'em out of the Springs." The intoxicated revelers' favorite prank was to sink a vehicle into the watery depths, which created a gruesome level of pollution. The WKPP project established a definitive link between the sink and the Wakulla Spring, leading to an impetus to clean up Cherokee Sink and regulate its use.[2]

Both environmentally sound burnings of the property and extensive clean-up efforts were necessary. In 2003, volunteers removed a car, a boat, a motorcycle, and truckloads of debris from the sinkhole's depths. For over a decade, prescribed burnings restored the land around the sink to its natural forest growth, and volunteers tended to native plants. From 2004–2007, boardwalks were built, erosion controls established, and gullies filled in. Cherokee Sink, though no longer a site for swimming, became the focus of a pleasant hike inside a little-seen portion of the park.[3]

Even as the rangers and volunteers worked to undo damage dating back a half-century, new threats were emerging, potential disasters tied to Florida's rapid development. Two related problems have plagued Wakulla Springs since the 1990s: the presence of hydrilla in the spring and the decline of Wakulla's water quality, which has darkened the once great "liquid bowl of light."

Scott Savery, the biologist for Wakulla Springs, first noticed hydrilla in the Wakulla Spring in March 1997. The aquatic plant is native to Sri Lanka and was brought to America in the 1950s as a novelty item for aquariums. A careless Tampa resident released it in a canal, and from there it has spread into ecosystems around the state. Aggressive and deadly, hydrilla grows at a terrifying rate, forming large mats that tangle across the surface of the water and block out sunlight, killing native plant species and damaging areas where fish spawn. Some hydrilla vines at Wakulla grew to 40–50 feet, "probably world championship hydrilla in terms of height." From 1999 to 2002, rangers fought a never-ending battle against the plant, yanking out millions of pounds of hydrilla by hand and with a mechanical harvester. In April 2002, the beleaguered staff reluctantly turned to a herbicide that kills the hydrilla leaves but does not attack the roots. Applied in the spring, the poison keeps the hydrilla under control for six to eight months, but can never completely cure the problem.[4]

Exactly how hydrilla reached the Wakulla Spring is unknown. Most often, hydrilla spreads when strands of it become entangled in the propellers of motorboats, which are then used in another lake or river. All outside watercraft are banned at Wakulla, eliminating this pathway of contamination. It is most likely that tourists spread hydrilla when they visited compromised swimming areas in the Panhandle and then unwittingly carried tiny fragments of the plant into Wakulla on their swim fins and toys. Signs now warn visitors to thoroughly check their aquatic gear before entering the water.[5]

Even more horrific than the hydrilla infestation is the strange darkening of Wakulla's waters. Tea-colored water can be a natural occurrence. Tannic acid, produced by rotting leaves, naturally washes through the cave system and into the spring during exceptionally rainy seasons. Letters from lodge managers first mention dark spring waters in the summer of 1945. Other periods of cloudiness were noted occasionally through the 1980s. The blackening of the spring meant cancelled glass bottom boat tours, which cut park revenue nearly in half. But by the 1990s, the phenomena could no longer be solely attributed to decaying leaves and heavy rain. In 1996, the glass bottom boats ran for 82 days of continuous operation from May until early August, which was the longest uninterrupted operational period since 1993. By 2015, the darkness had become so permanent that Henry, the famous "pole-vaulting fish," could no longer be seen performing his antics. His image was removed from a park sign he had inhabited for almost fifty years.[6]

At the same time the spring was turning dark, large mats of green algae were appearing on the bottom of the river and around the spring. Other North Florida springs were similarly affected by the green slime. A special Springs Task Force was initiated by Governor Jeb Bush to study the problem. Most experts attributed the unchecked algae growth to nitrate pollution seeping into the springs. Beneath the surface, Florida's limestone foundation is like Swiss cheese, riddled with holes and caves that allow contamination from one part of the region to flow into another. Seepage from lawn and agricultural fertilizers, as well as waste leaking from septic tanks and generated by wastewater spray fields and large livestock farms, goes down into the aquifer to be spit out by Florida's delicate springs. Tests easily demonstrated that nitrate pollution in the Wakulla Spring had increased five-fold since the 1960s. With more people, agriculture, and industry in the Panhandle has come greater pollution of Wakulla and other Florida springs. While the contamination of places like Cherokee Sink had been easy to pinpoint, reverse, and control, this form of pollution, originating from so many sources and more of an effect of growth rather than of harmful intent, is much harder to understand and prevent.[7]

In 2014, after an unpopular law requiring inspections of septic tanks had been rescinded, the Florida legislature finally took concrete action to try to save Florida's springs. Almost $75 million from the state and local governments was earmarked to improve water quality. Among the many projects were four designed specifically to improve the Wakulla basin by switching homes in the area from septic tanks to a central sewer. Governor Rick Scott vowed that if re-elected he would push for $50 million a year for more spring restoration projects. Whether these efforts will be successful, or continuously funded, remains to be seen.[8]

Another hopeful sign for water preservation was the

Florida Water and Land Conservation Initiative, Amendment 1, which appeared on the November 4, 2014 state ballot. This measure proposed to dedicate 33 percent of the net revenue from the existing excise tax on documents to the Land Acquisition Trust Fund (LAFT). Founded in 1963 primarily to buy land for parks and recreation areas, the LAFT had seen its budgets slashed since 2009. Supporters of Amendment 1, including former governors Charlie Crist and Bob Graham and the organization *Florida's Water and Land Legacy*, emphasized that the measure would "enhance drinking water, conservation, and recreation without raising taxes." Protecting the region's natural beauty, advocates of Amendment 1 argued, was also essential to protecting Florida's tourism industry. The measure passed by a vote of 4,238,739 to 1,415,924, or almost 75 percent to 25 percent. Amendment 1's long-term effects, and whether it will provide adequate funding for extension of state efforts to protect virtually all water resources, lie in the future.[9]

Water pollution is not the only current threat to the survival of Wakulla Springs. Economic and political decisions consistently endanger the park. The increasingly conservative political climate has intensified the debate between developers and environmentalists.

In 2012, Tallahassee Community College (TCC) received a $4 million grant from the state to build the Wakulla Environmental Institute (WEI) on 160 acres south of Crawfordville. TCC submitted a request to lease almost 2,000 acres in the Wakulla Springs State Park as part of its new project. The property would be transformed into an RV and tent campground, supposedly as a training facility for future park managers. A similar proposal had been floated in 2011 by the DEP. Its version included an equestrian area, but it had been halted by community objections.

The Wakulla business community embraced the WEI proposal, but environmentalists and concerned citizens immediately rallied against it, objecting to the campground's inevitable impact on the fragile spring and cave system. Opponents of WEI pointed out that existing public campgrounds were available within twenty minutes of the WEI campus. Jim Murdaugh, TCC's president, assured a public hearing that WEI's intent was to "create a world-class destination that brings together conservation, education and recreation in a manner that stimulates economic development in an environmentally sensitive way," but Jack Rudloe, veteran of many development-versus-conservation tussles, warned that the Creature from the Black Lagoon would be "infuriated" with the plan. A few months later, TCC withdrew its request.[10]

Management of the lodge has likewise raised concerns about maintaining the park's reputation and integrity. By 2010, many locals believed that the lodge was closing. Rumors that cost-cutting measures would lead to the shuttering of state parks were common. In 2011, the state decided to turn to private vendors in many of its holdings. Cape Leisure, a company with concessions at several state parks, was given the day-to-day operations of the Wakulla Springs Lodge, restaurant, and gift shop. In a year's time, Cape Leisure had gone through three general managers at the lodge and was working desperately to reconnect with the people of the county to correct the impression that the lodge had closed.[11] In November 2014, the lodge concession passed to Wakulla Hospitality, a company owned by eight prominent local businessmen. Numerous updates, including new furniture for the lobby and a renovation of the heat and air-conditioning system, were installed in 2015. Rechristened "The Lodge at Wakulla Springs," the property currently emphasizes its attractiveness as a wedding venue and family reunion site, as well as a quiet spot for the traditional family vacation. General Manager David Smith says that plans for future renovation include restoring the rooms to their original 1930s grandeur.[12]

Florida's state parks are among the finest in the nation, providing a glimpse of the "Real Florida" to all visitors. They are especially important recreational resources for lower-income families because of their modest fees. But at Wakulla and across the state, an almost constant effort to make the parks financially self-supporting endangers their management as well as their ecosystems. In 2015, the Florida legislature proposed bills to allow "low impact" agricultural uses by private interests in a number of parks, including Wakulla Springs. These could easily include cattle grazing and timber harvesting. While the bills did not become law in the spring of 2015, such threats loom large with every legislative session.[13]

Fortunately for Wakulla Springs, a group of concerned citizens has banded together to protect it. Formed in 1995, the Friends of Wakulla Springs is a nonprofit volunteer organization dedicated to educating the public about the park. The Friends serve as the park's most vocal advocacy group. Along with organizing educational talks and hikes, the Friends raise money for renovations and upkeep, and inform the county and state on issues affecting Wakulla and other Florida springs. They were essential in speaking out against proposed developments by Ken Kirton and TCC, and their leaders write frequent editorials urging voters to consider wetlands issues. The Friends of Wakulla Springs sweeten their love of the park with a healthy sense of humor; a number of their fundraisers have emphasized the Creature from the Black Lagoon. The Henry, one of the famous glass-bottom boats, has been re-purposed by the Friends as a floating classroom, in hopes that by taking students out onto the darkened spring waters, a new generation will be motivated to fight to clean them.[14]

. . . .

In 2013, Walt Disney World announced a new destination called Disney Springs. A major "reimagining" of Downtown Disney in Orlando, the area would feature restaurants, retail shops, and entertainment stages, all themed to an imaginary Florida town. Preview drawings of Disney Springs showed its vaguely Spanish architecture inspired by St. Augustine. In a promotional video, Theron Skees, Disney Imagineering Executive Creative Director, invited future guests to envision a "little green field" in Florida where a spring was found. Around this natural spring "a whole town was built on, and over time that town was converted into a retail, dining and entertainment venue that's something the world hasn't seen before." This revised aspect of the vast Walt Disney World Resort opened in 2016.[15]

Disney has its necessary place in Florida tourism. But Florida provides, naturally, far more breathtaking adventures and exquisite landscapes than anything Disney's imagineers could cook up in their magical laboratories. Wakulla Springs is real, a beautiful blue place in a deep green wood. It is a world of primordial wonders, where nature prevails and artifice is strictly limited. It is the watery Eden where Florida was born.

It would be shameful for Florida to lose Wakulla Springs or any of her amazing natural fountains. Future generations should not miss their chance to swim and play in a freshwater spring rather than a chlorinated pool, to see fish and birds and alligators that are flesh and blood creatures, not robots or holograms. But Florida's springs are in very real danger, from pollution, climate change, and politics. Floridians and their guests bear a tremendous responsibility to Wakulla and all of Florida's springs — to use them cautiously, to protect them fiercely, and to love them eternally.

Cherokee Sink, a pleasant hike in a little-seen portion of the park.
(Wakulla Springs State Park)

Tons of hydrilla have been removed from the Spring and river.
(Wakulla Springs State Park)

In 2015, Friends of Wakulla Springs gathered on the boat dock to celebrate 20 years of citizens' support for Wakulla Springs State Park. (Bob Thompson)

For information about joining the organization, go to www.wakullasprings.org.

ENDNOTES

Chapter 1

1. G. E. Ferguson, C. W. Lingham, S. K. Love, and R. O. Vernon, *Springs of Florida,* Florida Geological Survey, Geological Bulletin 31 (Tallahassee 1947), 4-7, 9, 169-171; Edward A. Fernald and Donald J. Patton, eds., *Water Resources Atlas of Florida* (Tallahassee: Florida State University, 1984), 43.

2. Alva Stone to Alan Whitehouse, 1 October 1991, Florida Park Service Archives, Tallahassee.

3. James Clarence Simpson, *A Provisional Gazetteer of Florida Place-Names of Indian Derivation Either Obsolescent or Retained Together With Other of Recent Application,* Florida Geological Survey, Special Publications No. 1 (Tallahassee 1956), 122; Bertha E. Bloodworth and Alton C. Morris, *Places in the Sun: The History and Romance of Florida Place-Names* (Gainesville: University Presses of Florida, 1978), 38-39; Thorn Bacon, "Do Not Disturb!," *All Florida Magazine,* 7 August 1966; Michael Wisenbaker, "Wakulla's Living Treasure," *The Real Florida,* Spring 1999, 23.

4. Stanely J. Olsen, "The Wakulla Cave," *Natural History,* August 1958, 401; Stephen C. Bryne, *Archaeological Survey at the Edward Ball Wakulla Springs State Park,* Bureau of Archaeological Research, Florida Archaeological Reports 6 (Tallahassee 1988), 15-22.

5. "The Narrative of Alvar Nunez Cabeza de Vaca" in Frederick W. Hodge and Theodore H. Lewis, eds., *Spanish Explorers in the Southern United States, 1528-1543* (1907; repr., New York: Barnes

& Noble, 1946), 21, 30-37; Clifton Paisley, *The Red Hills of Florida, 1528-1865* (Tuscaloosa: University of Alabama Press, 1989), 17.

6. John R. Swanton, *Final Report of the De Soto Expedition Commission* (Washington, D.C.: Government Printing Office, 1939), 114-15; Bryne, *Archaeological Survey,* 24; Calvin Jones, "July 1993 Tree Planting/Test Hole Project at the Probable 1528 Aute Apalachee Indian Site (Bear Site) in the Edward Ball Wakulla Springs State Park, Wakulla County, Florida," Bureau of Archaeological Research, Florida Division of Historical Resources, 6 September 1993, n.p.; "The Narrative of the Expedition of Hernando De Soto by the Gentleman of Elvas," in Hodge and Lewis, eds., *Spanish Explorers in the Southern United States,* 160-64; Paisley, *The Red Hills of Florida,* 18-22.

7. Paisley, *The Red Hills of Florida,* 24-25; James W. Covington, "Apalachee Indians, 1704-1763," *Florida Historical Quarterly* 50 (April 1972): 368; Michael Gannon, ed., *The New History of Florida* (Gainesville: University Press of Florida, 1996), 97; John H. Hann, *Apalachee: The Land Between the Rivers* (Gainesville: University Presses of Florida, 1988), 360; Bryne, *Archaeological Survey,* 24-27.

8. J. Leitch Wright, Jr., *The Only Land They Knew: The Tragic Story of Indians in the Old South* (New York: Free Press, 1981), 113-15; Mark F. Boyd, Hale G. Smith, and John W. Griffin, *Here They Once Stood: The Tragic End of the Apalachee Missions* (Gainesville: University of Florida Press, 1851), 90; Covington, "Apalachee Indians," 374-75.

9. Bryne, *Archeological Survey,* 28-30; Lawrence Kinnaird, "The Significance of William Augustus Bowles' Seizure of Panton's Apalachee Store in 1792," *Florida Historical Quarterly* 9 (January 1931): 156; J. Leitch Wright, Jr., *William Augustus Bowles, Director General of the Creek Nation* (Athens: University of Georgia Press, 1967), 65.

10. John Calhoun Upchurch, "Middle Florida: An Historical Geography of the Area Between the Apalachicola and Suwannee River" (Ph.D. diss., University of Tennessee, 1971), 78-79; Kinnaird, "The Significance of William Augustus Bowles' Seizure of Panton's Apalachee Store in 1792," 156-57, 170-76; Paisley, *The Red Hills of Florida,* 41-42.

11. Andrew Ellicott, *The Journal of Andrew Ellicott* (Phildelphia: Budd & Bartram, 1803), 238-40; Catherine Van Cortlandt Mathews, *Andrew Ellicott: His Life and Letters* (New York: The Grafton Press, 1908), 172-81; Mark F. Boyd, "The Fortifications at San Marcos de Apalachee," *Florida Historical Quarterly* 15 (July 1936): 20-21; Paisley, *The Red Hills of Florida,* 42-43.

12. Boyd, "The Fortifications at San Marcos de Apalachee," 19; Upchurch, "Middle Florida," 79-87.

13. James Parton, *Life of Andrew Jackson,* 3 vols. (New York: Mason Borthers, 1860), 2: 430-38, 454-59, 477-80; Paisley, The *Red Hills of Florida,* 52; T. Frederick Davis, "Milly Francis and Duncan McKrimmon: An Authentic Florida Pocahontas," *Florida Historical Quarterly* 21 (January 1943): 254; Bryne, Archaeological Survey, 28.

14. Bryne, *Archeological Survey,* 32.

15. William Darby, *Memoir on the Geography and Natural and Civil History of Florida* (Philadelphia: T. H. Palmer, 1821), n.p.

Chapter 2

1. Mary Louise Ellis and William Warren Rogers, *Tallahassee and Leon County: A History and Bibliography* (Tallahassee: Department of State, 1986), 4.

2. John Lee Williams, "Journal of an Expedition," *Pensacola Gazette & West Florida Advertiser,* 25 April, 5 June 1824; "The Selection of Tallahassee as the Capital: Journal of John Lee

Williams, Commissioner to Locate the Seat of Government of the Territory of Florida," *Florida Historical Quarterly* 1 (April 1908): 44; (July 1908): 18; John Lee Williams, *A View of West Florida* (1827; repr., Gainesville: University of Florida Press, 1976), 23, 27, 37, 106; John Lee Williams, *The Territory of Florida* (1837; repr., Gainesville: University of Florida Press, 1962), 147. There is some discrepancy on the exact date of Williams's survey of the Wakulla, but it most likely occurred before he met with Simmons.

3. Venila Lorina Shores, "Canal Projects of Territorial Florida," *Tallahassee Historical Society Annual* (1934-1935): 12-13; J. E. Dovell, *Florida: Historic, Dramatic, Contemporary* 3 vols. (New York: Lewis Historical Publishing Company, Inc., 1952), 3: 394.

4. Paisley, *The Red Hills of Florida,* 74, 82-88.

5. Tallahassee *Floridian & Advocate,* 8 September 1829.

6. Charles J. Latrobe, *The Rambler in North America* 2 vols. (New York, 1835), 2:37.

7. *Letters on Florida* (New York: J. Narine, 1835), 15.

8. Upchurch, "Middle Florida," 80-81; Lou Rich, "The History of Wakulla Spring," (Honors Paper, Florida State University, 1963), 6; Paisley, *The Red Hills of Florida,* 95.

9. Comte de Castelnau, "Essay on Middle Florida, 1837-1838," *Florida Historical Quarterly* 25 (January 1948), translation by Arthur R. Seymour, 199-200, 211; Comte de Castelnau, "Note Sur la Source de la Riviere de Wakulla dans la Floride," *Bulletin de la Societe de Geographic* 2 (1839): 242-47. A translation of this article is available in the P. K. Yonge Library, University of Florida, Gainesville.

10. Bryne, *Archaeological Survey,* 38; "The Wakulla. A Sketch From The Note-Book of a Clergyman," *Knickerbocker,* August 1841, 134-37.

11. Tallahassee *Star of Florida,* 25 May 1843; Rich, "The History of Wakulla Spring," 11.

12. Tallahassee *Floridian & Journal,* 25 May 1850.

13. Solon Robinson, "The Traveler, No. 5," *American Agriculturalist* 10 (May 1851): 148; E. S. Gaillard, "Medical Topography of Florida," No. 2 *Charleston Medical Journal and Review,* repr. in *DeBow's Review* 19 (November 1855): 554-55.

14. Charles Lanman, *Adventures in the Wilds of the United States and the British Provinces* 2 vols. (Philadelphia 1856), 2: 143-45; Fernandina *East Floridian,* 6 October 1859.

15. William Warren Rogers, ed., "Florida on the Eve of the Civil War as Seen by a Southern Reporter," *Florida Historical Quarterly* 39 (October 1960): 153-54; Charleston *Daily Courier,* 4 April 1861.

16. Deed Book 4 of Wakulla County Records (31 March 1855), 243; Deed Book AB of Wakulla County Records (5 January 1859), 372-73.

17. Ellis and Rogers, *Tallahassee and Leon County,* 14; Bryne, *Archaeological Survey,* 40, 45, 80.

Chapter 3

1. Bertram H. Groene, *Ante-Bellum Tallahassee* (Tallahassee: Florida Heritage Foundation, 1971), 165.

2. Tallahassee *Floridian & Journal,* 19 June 1858.

3. Deed Book CD of Wakulla County Records (11 July 1871), 36; Tallahassee *Weekly Floridian,* 15 April 1873.

4. Tallahassee *Weekly Floridian,* 6 May 1873, 31 March 1874.

5. "John L. Thomas of Wakulla Springs," *Magnolia Monthly* 7 (February 1969): n.p.; Deed Book CD of Wakulla County Records

(27 December 1875), 494; Deed Book EF of Wakulla County Records (31 January 1879), 9-10.

6.   Tallahassee *Weekly Floridian,* 8 February 1876.

7.   Ibid., 11 April 1882.

8.   Deed Book EF of Wakulla County Records (13 March 1882), 478; Tallahassee *Weekly Floridian,* 16 May 1882.

9.   Robinson, *Florida,* 189.

10.   Tallahassee *Weekly Floridian,* 10 December 1885.

11.   Ibid., 5 May 1887, 6 May 1891, 14 May 1892; Rich, "The History of Wakulla Spring," 41; Madeleine Carr, historian, interview by the author, 20 June 2001, Edward Ball Wakulla Springs State Park.

12.   Deed Book EF of Wakulla County Records (17 April 1886), 588; Deed Book GH of Wakulla County Records (1 December 1890), 348, (14 July 1891), 433-34; Deed Book 6 of Wakulla County Records (6 December 1909), 41; Deed Book 5 of Wakulla County Records (2 November 1907), 632; Deed Book 6 of Wakulla County Records (30 December 1909), 27; Deed Book 7 of Wakulla County Records (14 April 1915), 15; Deed Book 9 of Wakulla County Records (6 September 1915), 108.

13.   George Charlton Matson and Samuel Sanford, *Geology and Ground Waters of Florida* (Washington: U. S. Government Printing Office, 1913), 422; Herman Gunter, *Explorations for Gas and Oil in Florida* (Tallahassee: 1948), mimeographed, n. p.; Rich, "History of Wakulla Spring," 42-43.

14.   Tallahassee *Daily Democrat,* 10 October 1916; Deed Book 9 of Wakulla County Records (9 December 1919), 459; Deed Book 10 of Wakulla County Records (9 December 1919), 188.

15.   George Apthorp, "A Trip to Wakulla Springs," unpublished article, c. 1915, Florida Park Service Archives, Tallahassee.

16. Tallahassee *Daily Democrat,* 28 June 1923, reprinted from the *Albany Herald.*

17. Deed Book 13 of Wakulla County Records (3 October 1925), 375; Tallahassee *Daily Democrat* 14 June 1927; 7 October 1935.

18. B. K. Roberts, retired Florida Supreme Court Justice, interview by author, 7 September 1987, Tallahassee; Tallahassee *Daily Democrat,* 12 May 1923; 7, 10 May 1927; 7 May 1928; 30 April, 1 May 1931; 6 May 1934.

19. Tallahassee *Daily Democrat,* 2 September 1930.

20. Ibid., 22 February 1931.

21. Ibid., 15, 22 April, 5, 6, 27 May, 7, 8, 16 June 1931.

22. Ibid., 15 December 1933; 27 February, 12 March 1934.

23. Deed Book 18 of Wakulla County Records (7 May 1934), 395-96; (10 May 1934), 398.

24. *Tallahassee Democrat,* 25 June 1981; Jacksonville *Florida Times-Union,* 25 June 1981; Rich, "History of Wakulla Spring," 30; Tallahassee *Daily Democrat,* 6 September 1934.

Chapter 4

1. Tracy Revels, "Ed Ball: Last of the Robber Barons" in Lewis N. Wynne and James J. Horgan, eds., *Florida Pathfinders* (Saint Leo, Florida: Saint Leo College Press, 1994), 1-3. There are two biographies of Ed Ball, with titles that play on Ball's favorite toast: Raymond K. Mason and Virginia Harrison, *Confusion to the Enemy: A Biography of Ed Ball* (New York: Dodd, Mead and Company, 1976) and Leon Odell Griffith, *Ed Ball: Confusion to the Enemy* (Tampa: Trend House, 1975).

2. Marquis James, *Alfred I. DuPont: The Family Rebel* (Indianapolis: The Bobbs-Merrill Company, 1941), 398-401; Joseph

Frazier Wall, *Alfred I. duPont: The Man and His Family* (New York: Oxford University Press, 1990), 485; Richard Greening Hewlett, *Jessie Ball duPont* (Gainesville: University Press of Florida, 1992), 73-74.

3. Hewlett, Jessie Ball duPont, 105-13; *Miami Herald*, 31 July 1966; Burton Altman, "'In the Public Interest?' Ed Ball and the FEC Railway War," *Florida Historical Quarterly* 64 (July 1985): 32-47; Freeman Lincoln, "The Terrible Tempered Mr. Ball," *Fortune,* November 1952, 158.

4. *Vero Beach Press-Journal,* 13 July 1961; *Miami Herald,* 17 March 1968.

5. Rush Loving, Jr., "Ed Ball's Marvelous, Old-Style Money Machine," *Fortune,* December 1974, 170; Jacob C. Belin, Chairman of the St. Joe Paper Company, interview by author, 7 April 1988, Port St. Joe; Tracy E. Danese, *Claude Pepper and Ed Ball: Politics, Purpose, and Power* (Gainesville: University Press of Florida, 2000), 20.

6. Tallahassee *Daily Democrat,* 1 April, 19 September 1935; *Tallahassee Democrat,* 2 June 1989.

7. Robert L. Murray, Jr., Bookkeeper for Ed Ball, interview by Robin Sellers, 17 November 1999, Ed Ball Wakulla Springs State Park, transcript in Florida Park Service Archives, Tallahassee.

8. Tallahassee *Daily Democrat,* 3 January 1937; Davis and Campbell, eds., *Album of Florida and West Indies Hotels* (Miami Beach: Davis and Campbell, 1938), 153; DeWitt Lamb, "Wakulla Springs is Termed One of State's Chief Attractions," Jacksonville *Florida Times-Union,* 2 May 1938, 7.

9. A. P. Shoemaker, Jr., to A. L. Schlesinger, Jr., 16 March 1952. Florida Park Service Archives, Tallahassee.

10. *Tallahassee Democrat,* 13 December 1993.

11. Lorenz More, ed., *Florida Hotel and Travel Guide* (New York: Florida Guide Company, 1941), 368; Jacksonville *Florida Times-Union*, 31 August 1941; *Sanford Herald*, 6 May 1939.

12. Crawfordville *Wakulla News*, 26 February 1943; J. D. Harvey, Wakulla Springs Sales Director, interview by author, 17 August 1989, Edward Ball Wakulla Springs State Park.

13. Crawfordville *Wakulla News*, 17 June 1955; *Tallahassee Democrat*, 11 September 1960; 3 March 1963; Ocala *Star Banner*, 9 July 1961.

14. Hawk Jackson, Wakulla Springs boat guide, interview by author, 17 August 1989, Edward Ball Wakulla Springs State Park; Belin interview, 7 April 1988; Harvey interview, 17 August 1989.

15. *Tallahassee Democrat*, 5 March 1978.

16. Betty Watts, *The Watery Wilderness of Apalach, Florida* (Tallahassee: Apalach Books, 1975), 76-77; Harvey interview, 17 August 1989; Jacksonville *Florida Times-Union*, 13 March 1970; Crawfordville *Wakulla News*, 30 July 1970.

17. Crawfordville *Wakulla News*, 26 August, 7 October 1971. For a detailed consideration of Ball's legal battles to keep his fence, see "The River War" in Tracy J. Revels, *Watery Eden: A History of Wakulla Springs* (Tallahassee: Sentry Press, 2002).

18. *Tallahassee Democrat*, 30 June 1973; Crawfordville *Wakulla News*, 17 May 1973; Revels, *Watery Eden*, 60-68.

19. *Tallahassee Democrat*, 11, 14, 15 July 1975; 30 June, 11 July 1979; Tallahassee *Florida Flambeau*, 14 July 1975; 19, 23 July 1979; Crawfordville *Wakulla News*, 10 August 1976, 12 July 1979.

20. *Tallahassee Democrat*, 5 March 1978; *Miami Herald*, 4 February 1996.

21. *Tallahassee Democrat*, 25 June 1981; Crawfordville *Wakulla News*, 24 June 1981.

Chapter 5

1. Crawfordville *Wakulla News*, 24 September 1981; 7 July 1983; 21 February 1985; *Tallahassee Democrat*, 6 April 1985.

2. Jacksonville *Florida Times-Union*, 23 February 1972; Crawfordville *Wakulla News*, 11 April, 2 May 1985; *Tallahassee Democrat*, 1 May 1985.

3. Crawfordville *Wakulla News*, 13, 27 June 1985; *Tallahassee Democrat*, 6, 20 June, 3 July 1985.

4. *Tallahassee Democrat*, 31 July 1985.

5. *Tallahassee Democrat*, 12 April, 23 May, 26, 30 July 1986; Belin interview, 7 April 1988.

6. *Tallahassee Democrat*, 5 September, 2 October 1986; Crawfordville *Wakulla News*, 2 October 986; Harvey interview, 17 August 1989.

7. *Tallahassee Democrat*, 14, 15 July 1987; Tallahassee *Florida Flambeau*, 14, 16 July 1987; William C. Stone, ed., *The Wakulla Springs Project* (Austin: The U. S. Deep Caving Team, 1989), passim.

8. *Tallahassee Democrat*, 8 September 1993; Crawfordville *Wakulla News*, 5 May, 20 June, 9 September 1993; Carr interview, 20 June 2001. For a detailed study of Kirton's legal battles over his right to develop his property, see "The Korner War" in Revels, *Watery Eden*.

9. Crawfordville *Wakulla News*, 23 September 1993; 3 February, 24 March 1994; *Tallahassee Democrat*, 23 September 1993; Carr interview, 20 June 2001.

10. Crawfordville *Wakulla News*, 20 April 1995; *Tallahassee Democrat*, 2 May 1995.

11. *Tallahassee Democrat*, 10 May 1995; Crawfordville *Wakulla*

News, 25 May, 22 June 1995; *Florida Wildlife Fed'n v. Wakulla Co., Fl.*, 30 May 1995.

12.   *Tallahassee Democrat*, 19, 23 August, 18 October 1995; Carr interview, 20 June 2001; Crawfordville *Wakulla News*, 31 August, 14 September, 12, 14 October 1995.

13.   Crawfordville *Wakulla News*, 19 October, 14 December 1995; 8, 15, 22 May, 12 June 1997; 15, 29 June 1998; *Tallahassee Democrat*, 19 June 1997; 14 January 1998.

14.   *Florida Wildlife Fed'n v. Wakulla Co., Fl.*, 23 May 1997; Craw-fordville *Wakulla News*, 29 May 1997; *Kirton v. Florida Wildlife Fed'n*, 706 So. 2d 290 (Fla. 1st DCA 1998).

15.   Crawfordville *Wakulla News*, 1 April, 17 June, 28 October 1999; 18 May 2000.

16.   *Tallahassee Democrat*, 21 July 1999; "Wakulla Springs," *Florida Fish and Wildlife News*, 20 November 1999; Department of Environmental Protection Communications Office Press Release, 20 July 1999.

17.   Crawfordville *Wakulla News*, 25 May 2000.

Chapter 6

1.   T. Frederick Davis, "Juan Ponce De Leon's Voyages to Florida," *Florida Historical Quarterly* 15 (July 1935): 25, 46-47.

2.   *Wakulla Springs: Land of Romance and Mystery* (Garden City: Doubleday One Dollar Book Club, n.d.), 2-4

3.   Lanman, *Adventures in the Wilds*, 2: 145.

4.   Davis, "Milly Francis and Duncan McKrimmon: An Authentic Florida Pocahontas," 245-65; Paisley, *The Red Hills of Florida*, 53-54.

5. *Port St. Joe Star*, 12 July 1973; Tallahassee *Florida Sentinel*, 18 June 1850; *Wakulla Springs: Land of Romance and Mystery*, n.p.; Tallahassee *Weekly Floridian*, 15 April 1873.

6. Crawfordville *Wakulla News*, 18 January 1979.

7. Irving A. Leonard,. *The Florida Adventure of Kirk Munroe* (Chuluota, Florida: The Mickler House, 1975), 1-7; Kirk Munroe, *Wakulla* (New York: Harper, 1886), passim.

8. Mary Bethel Alfriend, *San Luis of Apalachee* (Boston: Chapman & Grimes, 1939), 234; Mary Bethel Alfried, *Juan Ortiz: Gentleman of Seville* (Boston: Chapman & Grimes, 1940), 152-55.

9. *Tallahassee Democrat*, 10 November 1993, 4 June 2001; Jack Yaeger, Jr., *Smiling Jack Yaeger* (Tallahassee: Ellie Whitney Yaeger, 1997), 23; Russ Franklin, "Strong Like Johnny Weissmuller" (Ph.D. diss., Florida State University, 1999), 172-75.

10. www.friendsofbooks.com/store/murder-wakulla-springs-book-187480.html (accessed 22 June 2015); http://io9.com/marvel-at-the-winners-of-the-2014-world-fantasy-awards-1656598260 (accessed 22 June 2015).

11. Tallahassee *Floridian and Advocate*, 19 May 1849; Reinette Gamble Long, "Legend of Wakulla," in *Osola; A Florida Epic: The Legend of the Mysterious Smoke of Wakulla*, 2nd ed. (Tallahassee: 1922), n.p.; Rich, "The History of Wakulla Spring," 38-40.

12. Leon Stokesbury, "Wakulla Spring" in *Wakulla Portraits: Poetry & Photography* (Tallahassee: Tallahassee Community College, 1983), n.p.

13. *St. Petersburg Times*, 18 September 1960; Andrew H. Blount, "Watercolorists Mary Jo Weale," Florida Park Service Archives, Tallahassee; Tallahassee *Capitol Outlook*, 10 September 1987; *Tallahassee Democrat*, 15 June 1996.

14. *Camp Gordon Johnston Amphibian*, 24 April, 17 July 1943; Richard Shale, compiler, *Academy Awards*, 2nd ed. (New York:

Frederick Ungar Publishing, 1982), 361.

15. *Miami Herald*, 17 November 1946; Walt Lee, compiler, *Reference Guide to Fantasy Films* 3 vols. (Los Angeles: Chelsea-Lee Books, 1974) 2: n.p.; *Tallahassee Democrat*, 29 April 1990; Tallahassee *Daily Democrat*, 12 June 1941; 22 June 1984; 29 April 1990; Crawfordville *Wakulla News*, 18 July 1989.

16. Crawfordville *Wakulla News*, 23 June 1944; Tallahassee *Daily Democrat*, 1 April 1945; *Orlando Sentinel*, 9 October 1945; Robert E. Ellsworth, "The Pole-Vaulting Fish of Wakulla," *Holiday*, October 1946, 130-33; *Tallahassee Democrat*, 25 November 1987.

17. Richard Alan Nelson, *Lights! Camera! Florida!* (Tampa: Florida Endowment for the Humanities, 1987), 62; R. LeMoyne Cash, *Sportsmen's Annual: Wakulla County, Florida, 1954* (Tallahassee: R. LeMoyne Cash, 1954), 15; Leonard Wolf, *Horror: A Connoisseur's Guide to Literature and Film* (New York: Facts on File, 1989), 49, 187; John Stanley, *The Creature Features Movie Guide* (Pacifica, California: Creatures at Large, 1981), 44; Crawfordville *Wakulla News*, 16 September 1955; Ron Sachs, "A Creature Feature," *Miami Magazine*, August 1979, 8.

18. *Tallahassee Democrat*, 5 September 1965.

19. Crawfordville *Wakulla News*, 5 August 1976; *Tampa Tribune*, 1 April 1977.

20. Crawfordville *Wakulla News*, 11, 18 November 1976; *Tallahassee Democrat*, 14, 21 November 1976; *Tampa Tribune*, 21 November 1976.

21. Crawfordville *Wakulla News*, 5 August 1999.

Chapter 7

1. Ellicott, *The Journal of Andrew Ellicott*, 238-40; Mathews, *Andrew Ellicott*, 127-29; Boyd and Ponton, eds., "A Topographical

Memoir," 16-17, 40-41; Williams, *The Territory of Florida*, 147.

2. Castelnau, "Essay on Middle," 199; Castelnau, "Note sur la Source," 242-47.

3. Tallahassee *Floridian and Journal*, 25 May 1850.

4. Tallahassee Florida Sentinel, 18 June 1850; E. H. Sellards, *Florida Geological Survey Eighth Annual Report*, Florida Geological Survey (Tallahassee 1916), 104-04; George M. Barbour, *Florida for Tourists, Invalids, and Settlers* (New York: D. Appleton and Company, 1882), 84-85; Phillip Gerrell, archaeologist, interview by author, 14 December 1989, Florida State University; Tallahassee *Weekly Floridian*, 17 October 1902; Herman Gunter, "Once Roamed Land of Sunshine," *Florida Highways*, August 1941, 35-36.

5. Tallahassee *Daily Democrat*, 16 November 1930; Herman Gunter, "The Mastodon From Wakulla Springs," *Florida Woods and Waters*, Spring 1931, 15; Gunter, "Once Roamed," 35-36.

6. Robert Forrest Burgess, *The Cave Divers* (New York: Dodd & Mead, 1976), 80-84.

7. *Tallahassee Democrat*, 10 January 1965; Burgess, *The Cave Divers*, 84-91; Stanley J. Olsen, "The Wakulla Cave," *Natural History* 67 (August 1958): 398, 401-02.

8. *Tallahassee Democrat*, 6 August 1945; 9 February 1961; 27 May 1963; 30 June 1968; Jacksonville *Florida Times-Union*, 1 July 1968.

9. Stone, *The Wakulla Springs Project*, passim; *Tallahassee Democrat*, 31 October 1987; Crawfordville Wakulla News, 5 November 1987.

10. Tallahassee *Florida Flambeau*, 2 November 1987; 19 February 1988; Stone, *The Wakulla Springs Project*, iii, 123, 160; Crawfordville *Wakulla News*, 15 June 1984.

11. Michael Wisenbaker, "The WKPP Team," *Immersed*, Winter

1997, 10-14; Michael Wisenbaker, "Unraveling the Mysteries of the Maze," *NSS News*, July 1999, 196-98; *Miami Herald*, 22 February 2001.

12. *Miami Herald*, 6 October 1988; Bill Breen, "Quiet, Dark & Very Scary," *Reader's Digest*, June 2001, 91.

13. Barbara Ende, "Wakulla 2 – Building the First Fully 3D Cave Map," *NSS News*, September 2000, 245-52.

14. Ibid., 253-60, 270; *Tallahassee Democrat*, 28 October 1996; 20 June 1998; *Miami Herald*, 22 February 2001; Crawfordville *Wakulla News*, 15 June 2000.

15. Bryne, *Archaeological Survey*, 1.

16. Crawfordville *Wakulla News*, 13 January, 21 June 2000; Calvin Jones, "July 1993 Tree Planting/Test Hole Project at the Probably 1528 Aute Apalachee Indian Site (Bear Site) in the Edward Ball Wakulla Springs State Park, Wakulla County, Florida." Bureau of Archaeological Research, Florida Division of Historical Resources, 6 September 1993, n.p.

17. *Tallahassee Democrat*, 25 January 1995; Crawfordville *Wakulla News*, 26 January 1995, "Major Paleo Find in Wakulla Trench," *Florida Anthropological Society Newsletter*, March 1995, 3; *Tampa Tribune*, 26 January 1995.

18. *Tallahassee Democrat*, 17 February 1998; Crawfordville *Wakulla News*, 27 January 2000.

Chapter 8

1. Ibid, 8 September, 29 December 1994; 3 July 1997; Bill Roberts, "Wakulla Springs: Restored to Glory," *Wakulla Area Digest*, February 1998, 1.

2. *Tallahassee Democrat*, 26 February 2001.

3.   Ibid, 16 June 2014.

4.   Judith Ludlow and Scott Savery, "Hydrilla in Wakulla Springs State Park: The Battle Between Two Non-Indigenous Plants," *Aquatics*, Winter 1997, 15-16; Crawfordville *Wakulla News*, 25 September 1997.

5.   Ludlow and Savery, "Hydrilla," 15-16.

6.   Newton Perry, Wakulla Springs, to Edward Ball, Jacksonville, 13 September 1945; 17 January, 18 March 1946, letter on file, Florida Park Service Archives; *Tallahassee Democrat*, 26 August 1996, 25 December 2015.

7.   *Tallahassee Democrat*, 21 June 2000; 18 June 2006.

8.   Ibid, 22 January, 21 February, 8 August, 10 September 2014.

9.   https://ballotpedia.org/Florida_Water_and_Land_Conservation_Initiative,_Amendmant_1_(2014), (accessed 14 January 2016).

10.   Ibid, 19 June, 25 July 2014.

11.   Crawfordville *Wakulla News*, 19 September 2012.

12.   David Smith, General Manager of the Lodge at Wakulla Springs, phone interview with author, February 5, 2016.

13.   *Tallahassee Democrat*, 9 May 2015.

14.   Ibid, 30 July 1996; 27 October 1998; 25 December 2015.

15.   Ibid, 22 August 2014; *Orlando Sentinel*, 26 March 2015; https://disneyworld.disney.go.com/destinations/disney-springs/, (accessed April 8, 2016).

BIBLIOGRAPHY

Articles

Altman, Burton. "'In the Public Interest?' Ed Ball and the FEC Railway War." *Florida Historical Quarterly* 64 (July 1985): 32-47.

Apthorp, George. "A Trip to Wakulla Springs." c. 1915. Unpublished article on file at the Florida Park Services Archives, Tallahassee.

Bacon, Thorn. "Do Not Disturb!" *All Florida Magazine*, 7 August 1978, 15-17.

Blount, Andrea H. "Watercolorist Mary Jo Weale." Article on file at the Florida Park Services Archives, Tallahassee.

Boyd, Mark. F. "The Fortifications at San Marco de Apalache." *Florida Historical Quarterly* 15 (July 1936): 3-34.

Breen, Bill. "Quiet, Dark & Very Scary." *Reader's Digest*, June 2001, 86-95.

Castelnau, Comte de. "Essay on Middle Florida, 1837-1838," translated by Arthur R. Seymour. *Florida Historical Quarterly* 25 (January 1948): 199-255.

_____. "Note sur la source de la Riviere de Wakulla dans la Floride." Bulletin de la Societe de Geographic 2 (1839): 242-247.

Covington, James W. "Apalachee Indians, 1704-1763." *Florida Historical Quarterly* 50 (April 1972): 366-384.

Davis, T. Frederick. "Juan Ponce De Leon's Voyages to Florida." *Florida Historical Quarterly* 14 (July 1935): 8-66.

_____. "Milly Francis and Duncan McKrimmon: An Authentic Florida Pocahontas." *Florida Historical Quarterly* 21 (January 1943): 254-256.

Ellsworth, Robert E. "The Pole-Vaulting Fish of Wakulla." *Holiday*, October 1946, 130-133.

Ende, Barbara am. "Wakulla 2 – Building the First Fully 3D Cave Map." *NSS News*, September 2000, 244-260, 270.

"Four Rich, Rugged Individuals." *Newsweek*, 14 February 1972, 76-78.

Gaillard, E. S. "Medical Topography of Florida." *DeBow's Review* 19 (November 1855): 539-557.

Gunter, Herman. "Once Roamed Land of Sunshine." *Florida Highways*, August 1941, 13, 25-36.

_____. "The Mastodon From Wakulla Springs." *Florida Woods and Waters*, Spring 1931, 14-16.

Jackson, Lena E. "Sidney Lanier in Florida." *Florida Historical Quarterly*. 15 (October 1936): 118-124.

"John L. Thomas of Wakulla Springs." *Magnolia Monthly*, February 1969, n.p.

Jones, Calvin. "July 1993 Tree Planting/Test Hole Project at the Probably 1528 Aute Apalache Indian Site (Bear Site) in the Edward Ball Wakulla Springs State Park, Wakulla County, Florida." Bureau of Archaeological Research, Florida Division of Historical Resources, 6 September 1993, n.p.

Kinnaird, Lawrence. "The Significance of William Augustus Bowles' Seizure of Panton's Apalachee Store in 1792." *Florida Historical Quarterly* 9 (January 1931): 156-192.

Lincoln, Freeman. "The Terrible-Tempered Mr. Ball." Fortune, *November* 1952, 143-162.

Loving, Rush, Jr. "Ed Ball's Marvelous, Old-Style Money Machine." *Fortune*, December 1974, 170-185.

Ludlow, Judith and Savery, Scott. "Hydrilla in Wakulla Springs State Park: The Battle Between Two Non-Indigenous Plants." *Aquatics*, Winter 1997, 15-16.

"Major Paleo Finds in Wakulla Trench." *Florida Anthropological Society Newsletter*, March 1995, 3.

Olsen, Stanley J. "The Wakulla Cave." *Natural History* 67 (August 1958): 396-398, 401-403.

Reid, Randy. "The Return of a Tradition." *Wakulla Area Digest*, November 1955, 1, 12, 19, 38.

Robinson, Solon. "The Traveler, No. 5." *American Agriculturalist* 10 (May 1851): 147-149.

Rogers, William Warren, ed. "Florida on the Eve of the Civil War as Seen by a Southern Reporter." *Florida Historical Quarterly* 39 (October 1960): 145-158.

Sachs, Ron. "A Creature Feature." *Miami Magazine*, August 1979, 8.

Shores, Venila Lorina. "Canal Projects of Territorial Florida." *Tallahassee Historical Society Annual* (1934-1935): 12-18.

"The Selection of Tallahassee as the Capitol: Journal of John Lee Williams, Commission to Locate the Seat of Government of the Territory of Florida." *Florida Historical Quarterly* 1 (April 1908) 1-44, (July 1908), 1-50.

"The Wakulla. A Sketch From the Note-Book of a Clergyman." *Knickerbocker*, August 1841, 134-137.

"Wakulla Springs." *Florida Fish and Wildlife News*, 20 November 1999, n.p.

Wisenbaker, Michael. "The WKPP Team." *Immersed*, Winter 1997, 10-14.

_____. "Unraveling the Mysteries of the Maze." *NSS News*. July 1997, 196-199, 214.

_____. "Wakulla's Living Treasure." *The Real Florida*, Spring 1999, 22-25.

Books

Album of Florida and West Indies Hotels. Miami Beach: Davis and Campbell, 1938.

Alfriend, Mary Bethel. *Juan Ortiz: Gentleman of Seville*. Boston: Chapman & Grimes, 1940.

_____. *San Luis de Apalachee*. Boston: Chapman & Grimes, 1939.

Barbour, George M. *Florida for Tourists, Invalids and Settlers*. New York: D. Appleton and Company, 1882.

Bloodsworth, Bertha E. and Morris, Alton C. *Places in the Sun: The History and Romance of Florida Place Names*. Gainesville: University of Florida Press, 1978.

Boyd, Mark F.; Smile, Hale G., and Griffin, John W. *Here They Once Stood: The Tragic End of the Apalachee Missions*. Gainesville: University of Florida Press, 1951.

Bryne, Stephen C. *Archaeological Survey at the Edward Ball Wakulla Springs State Park*. Bureau of Archeological Research Reports 6. Tallahassee, 1988.

Burgess, Robert Forrest. *The Cave Divers.* New York: Dodd & Mead, 1976.

Cash, R. LeMoyne. *Sportsmen's Annual: Wakulla County, Florida, 1954.* Tallahassee: R. LeMoyne Cash, 1954.

Danese, Tracy E. *Claude Pepper and Ed Ball: Politics, Purpose, and Power.* Gainesville: University Press of Florida, 2000.

Darby, William. *Memoir on the Geography and the Natural and Civil History of Florida.* Philadelphia: T. H. Palmer, 1821.

Dovell, J. E. *Florida: Historic, Dramatic, Contemporary.* 3 vols. New York: Lewis Historic Publishing Company, Inc., 1952. Vol. 3.

Ellicott, Andrew. *The Journal of Andrew Ellicott.* Philadelphia: Budd and Bartram, 1803.

Ellis, Mary Louise and Rogers, William Warren. *Tallahassee and Leon County: A History and Bibliography.* Tallahassee: Florida Department of State, 1986.

Ferguson, G. E.; Lingham, C. W.; Love, S. K., and Vernon, R. O. *Springs of Florida.* Florida Geological Survey, Geological Bulletin 31. Tallahassee: 1947.

Fernald, Edward A. and Patton, Donald J., eds. *Water Resources Atlas of Florida.* Tallahassee: Florida State University, 1984.

Gannon, Michael, ed. *The New History of Florida.* Gainesville: University Press of Florida, 1996.

Griffin, Leon Odell. *Ed Ball: Confusion to the Enemy.* Tampa: Trend House, 1975.

Groene, Bertram. *Ante-Bellum Tallahassee.* Tallahassee: Florida Heritage Foundation, 1971.

Gunter, Herman. *Explorations for Gas and Oil in Florida.* Tallahassee: 1948.

Hann, John H. *Apalachee: The Land Between the Rivers.* Gainesville: University Presses of Florida, 1988.

Hewlett, Richard Greening. *Jessie Ball DuPont.* Gainesville: University Press of Florida, 1992.

Hodge, Fredrick W. and Lewis, Theodore H., eds. *Spanish Explorers in the Southern United States, 1528-1543.* 1907; reprint edition, New York: Barnes & Noble, 1946.

James, Marquis. *Alfred I. DuPont: The Family Rebel.* Indianapolis: The Bobbs Merrill Company, 1941.

Lanier, Sidney. *Florida: Its Scenery, Climate, and History.* Philadelphia: Lippincott, 1875.

Lanman, Charles. *Adventures in the Wilds of the United States and the British Provinces.* 2 vols. New York: 1856. Vol. 2.

Latrobe, Charles J. *The Rambler in North America.* 2 vols. New York: 1835. Vol. 2.

Lee, Walt, compiler. *Reference Guide to Fantasy Films.* 3 vols. Los Angeles: Chelsea-Lee Books, 1974. Vol. 2

Leonard, Irving A. *The Florida Adventures of Kirk Munroe.* Chuluota, Florida: The Mickler House, 1975.

Letters on Florida. New York: J. Narine, printer, 1835.

Long, Reinette Gamble. *Osola, A Florida Epic: The Legend of the Mysterious Smoke of Wakulla.* 2nd ed. Tallahassee, 1922.

Mason, Raymond K. and Harrison, Virginia. *Confusion to the Enemy: A Biography of Ed Ball.* New York: Dodd, Mead and Company, 1976.

Mathews, Catherine Van Cortlandt. *Andrew Ellicott: His Life and Letters.* New York: The Grafton Press, 1908.

Matson, George Charlton and Sanford, Samuel. *Geology and Ground Waters of Florida.* Washington: U. S. Government Printing Office, 1913.

More, Lorenz, ed. *Florida Hotel and Travel Guide.* New York: Florida Guide Company, 1941.

Morris, Allen. *Florida Place Names.* Coral Gables: University of Miami Press, 1974.

Munroe, Kirk. *Wakulla.* New York: Harper, 1886.

Nelson, Richard Alan. *Lights! Camera! Florida!.* Tampa: Florida Endowment for the Humanities, 1987.

Paisley, Clifton. *The Red Hills of Florida, 1528-1865.* Tuscaloosa: University of Alabama Press, 1989.

Parton, James. *Life of Andrew Jackson.* 3 vols. New York: Mason Brothers, 1860. Vol. 2.

Revels, Tracy J. *Watery Eden: A History of Wakulla Springs.* Tallahassee: Sentry Press, 2002.

Robinson, A. A. *Florida: A Pamphlet Descriptive of Its History, Topography, Climate, Soil, Resources, and Natural Advantages.* Tallahassee: Floridian Book and Job Office, 1882, 192.

Sellards, E. H. *Florida Geological Survey Eighth Annual Report.* Tallahassee: Florida Geological Survey, 1916.

Shale, Richard, compiler. *Academy Awards.* 2nd ed. New York: Frederick Ungar Publishing, 1982.

Simpson, James Clarence. *A Provisional Gazetteer of Florida Place-names of Indian Derivation Either Obsolescent or Retained Together With Others of Recent Application.* Florid Geological Survey, Special Publications No. 1. Tallahassee, 1956.

Stanley, John. *The Creature Features Movie Guide.* Pacifica, California: Creatures at Large, 1981.

Stone, William C., ed. T*he Wakulla Springs Project.* Austin: The U. S. Deep Caving Team, 1989.

Swanton, John R. *Final Report of the De Soto Expedition Commission.* Washington, D.C.: Government Printing Office, 1939.

Wakulla Portraits: Poetry & Photographs. Tallahassee: Tallahassee Community College, 1983.

Wakulla Springs: Land of Romance and Mystery. Garden City: Doubleday One Dollar Book Club, n.d.

Wall, Joseph Frazier. *Alfred I. duPont: the Man and His Family.* New York: Oxford University Press, 1990.

Watts, Betty. *The Watery Wilderness of Apalach, Florida.* Tallahassee: Apalach Book, 1975.

Williams, John Lee. *A View of West Florida.* 1827; reprint edition, Gainesville: University of Florida Press, 1976.

_____. *The Territory of Florida.* 1837; reprint edition, Gainesville: University of Florida Press, 1962.

Wolfe, Leonard. *Horror: A Connoisseur's Guide to Literature and Film.* New York: Facts on File, 1989.

Wright, J. Leitch, Jr. *The Only Land They Knew: The Tragic Story of the Indians in the Old South.* New York: Free Press, 1981.

_____. *William Augustus Bowles, Director General of the Creek Nation.* Athens: University of Georgia Press, 1967.

Wynne, Lewis N. and Horgan, James J., eds. *Florida Pathfinders.* Saint Leo, Florida: Saint Leo College Press, 1994.

Yaeger, Jack, Jr. *Smiling Jack Yaeger*. Tallahassee: Ellie Whitney
Yaeger, 1977.

Correspondence

Perry, Newton, Wakulla Springs to Edward Ball, Jacksonville, 13
September 1945; 17 January, 18 March 1946. Letter on file,
Florida Park Service Archives, Tallahassee.

Shoemaker, A. P., Jr., Edgewater Gulf Hotel to A. L. Schlesinger,
Jr., New Orleans, 16 May 1952. Letter on file, Florida Park
Service Archives, Tallahassee.

Stone, Alva to Alan Whitehouse, 1 October 1991. Letter on file,
Florida Park Service Archives, Tallahassee.

Dissertations, Theses, and Papers

Franklin, Russ. "Strong Like Johnny Weissmuller." Ph.D.
dissertation: Florida State University, 1999.

Rich, Lou. "The History of Wakulla Spring." Honors Paper:
Florida State University, 1963.

Upchurch, John Calhoun. "Middle Florida: An Historical
Geography of the Area Between the Apalachicola and
Suwannee Rivers." Ph. D. dissertation: University of
Tennessee, 1971.

Electronic Sources

http://io9.com/marvel-at-the-winners-of-the-2014-world-fantasy-
awards-1656598260

https://ballotpedia.org/Florida_Water_and_Land_Conservation_
Initiative,_Amendment_1_(2014)

https://disneyworld.disney.go.com/destinations/disney-springs/

www.friendsofbooks.com/store/murder-wakulla-springs-book-187480.html

Interviews

Belin, Jacob C. Chairman of the St. Joe Paper Company, Port St. Joe, Florida. 7 April 1988.

Carr, Madeleine. Historian, Edward Ball Wakulla Springs State Park, Florida. 20 June 2001.

Gerrell, Phillip. Archeologist, Tallahassee, Florida. 14 December 1989.

Harvey, J. D. Wakulla Springs Sales Director, Edward Ball Wakulla Springs State Park, Florida. 17 August 1989.

Jackson, Hawk. Park Ranger and Boat Guide, Edward Ball Wakulla Springs State Park, Florida. 17 August 1989.

Murray, Robert L. Bookkeeper. Interview by Robin Sellers, Wakulla Springs Lodge, 17 November 1999. Transcript on file, Florida Park Services Archives, Tallahassee.

Roberts, B. K. Retired Florida Supreme Court Justice, Tallahassee, Florida. 7 September 1989.

Smith, David. General Manager of the Lodge at Wakulla Springs. Phone interview. 5 February 2016.

Newspapers

Camp Gordon Johnston Amphibian

Charleston Daily Courier

Crawfordville Wakulla News

Fernandina East Floridian

Jacksonville Florida Times-Union

Miami Herald

Ocala Star Banner

Orlando Sentinel

Pensacola Gazette & West Florida Advertiser

Port St. Joe Star

Sanford Herald

St. Petersburg Times

Tallahassee Capitol Outlook

Tallahassee Daily Democrat

Tallahassee Florida Flambeau

Tallahassee Florida Sentinel

Tallahassee Floridian & Advocate

Tallahassee Floridian & Journal

Tallahassee Star of Florida

Tallahassee Weekly Floridian

Tampa Tribune

Vero Beach Press-Journal

Legal Documents

Deed Books, 1855-1934. Wakulla County Courthouse,
    Crawfordville, Florida.

INDEX

A

Abrams, M. D., 55
African Americans, 2, 26, 28, 35, 36
Alfriend, Mary Bethel, 55
Apalachee (Native American tribe), 4, 5, 53
Apalachee (region), 4, 5, 7, 8
Apalachicola Land Company, 7, 16, 19, 66
Apalachicola River, 6, 7
Aute, 3, 4, 70

B

Balchunas, Charles, 56
Ball, Edward (Ed), 30, 31, 33–39, 43, 45, 57, 67, 70, 78
Bowles, William Augustus, 5, 6
Browning, Rico, 58

C

Cape Leisure, 82
Cherokee Sink, 2, 78, 80
Christie, George T., 28, 29, 30
Crawfordville, 3, 37, 81
Creature From the Black Lagoon (character), 82, 83
Creature From the Black Lagoon (film), 58
Creeks (Native American tribe), 2, 4–7, 53, 54
Cypress Gardens, 36, 37

D

E

F

G

M

MacFarland, James, 44
Mainella, Fran P., 47, 78
Mastodon bones, 18, 29, 30, 66, 67, 71
Middle Florida, 8, 16, 23
Morrill, Thomas A., 38, 39
Motion pictures (filmed at Wakulla Springs), 29, 30, 56–60
Munroe, Kirk, 25, 55
Murdaugh, Jim, 81, 82

N

Narvaez, Panfilo de, 3
Nemours Foundation, 34, 39, 43
Newport (Florida), 24, 25

P

Panton, Leslie and Company, 5, 6
Perry, Newton, 36, 57, 58
Phillips, Florence Slosson, 27, 28
Phillips, Henry D., 27
Pope, Dick, 37
Port, Francis de la, Comte de Castelnau, 16, 65, 66

R

Rainbow Spring, 1
Rainbow Springs (tourist attraction), 37
Randall, P., 17, 24
Rudloe, Jack, 38, 82

S

T

U

United States Deep Caving Team, 68, 69

V

Vaca, Cabeza de, 3, 4

W

Wakulla Cave, 67–71
Wakulla County, 19, 23, 26, 37, 44, 45, 48, 57
Wakulla Environmental Institute (WEI), 81, 82
Wakulla Hospitality, 82
Wakulla River, 1, 3, 5–9, 14–16, 18, 19, 24, 31, 33, 38, 39, 43, 58, 65;
    fence controversy, 38, 39, 43
Wakulla Springs Dive Project, 45
Wakulla Springs Lodge, 1, 35-37, 44, 57, 58, 60, 71, 77, 82
Wakulla Springs May Picnic, 26, 27, 29
Wakulla Volcano, 55, 56
Water quality, 78–80
Weale, Mary Jo, 56
Weeki Wachee Spring, 1
Weeki Wachee Springs (tourist attraction), 36, 58
Weissmuller, Johnny, 57
Williams, John Lee, 13, 14, 65
Woodville Karst Plain Project (WKPP), 68–70, 78

Y

Young, Hugh, 8, 65